Ronan Powell

KS3
Maths, Science and English
Practice Tests

As you get towards the end of Key Stage 3, your school is likely to set you some tests to find out how you're doing in Maths, Science and English.

Happily, this CGP book is packed with practice tests for all three subjects so that you can go into the real tests fully prepared. We've even included detailed answers so that you can mark your own work.

What CGP is all about

Our sole aim here at CGP is to produce the highest quality books — carefully written, immaculately presented and dangerously close to being funny.

Then we work our socks off to get them out to you — at the cheapest possible prices.

Contents

ANSWERS

READING PAPER PULL-OUT

> The Reading Paper Pull-out is located at the back of this book.
> You'll need it for the English Reading Papers.

Published by CGP

Editors:
Rachael Rogers, Sophie Scott, Hayley Thompson, Matt Topping.

Contributors:
Cath Brown, Jane Chow, Paddy Gannon, Rebecca Harvey, Frederick Langridge,
Elisabeth Sanderson, Kieran Wardell, Jim Wilson, Nicola Woodfin.

With thanks to Matteo Orsini Jones and Sabrina Robinson for the proofreading.
With thanks to Laura Jakubowski for the copyright research.

ISBN: 978 1 84762 256 3

Clipart from Corel®
Printed by Elanders Ltd, Newcastle upon Tyne

How to Use This Book

This book contains loads of practice papers for Key Stage 3 Maths, Science and English.

Understandably you're desperate to get started, but just hold your horses —
there are **a few things you should know** first:

Here's What This Book Contains...

There are **three** sets of papers for each of the three subjects — Maths, Science and English.
There are **answers** for all the questions and **mark schemes** at the back of the book.
Use these to mark your work **after** you've had a go at the papers.

This is what's included in **each set** of papers:

Subject	Paper		Time Allowed	Marks Available
Maths	Paper A (no calculator)		1 hour	60
	Paper B (calculator)		1 hour	60
Science	Paper A		1 hour	75
	Paper B		1 hour	75
English	Reading Paper		15 minutes reading time, 1 hour writing time	32
	Writing Paper	Section A	15 minutes planning time, 30 minutes writing time	30 (goes towards overall Writing score)
		Section B	30 minutes writing time	20 (goes towards overall Writing score)
	Shakespeare Paper		45 minutes	18

Each English **Reading Paper** has **three** bits of **writing** for you to read and answer questions on.
These bits of writing are all in a **pull-out Reading Booklet** at the **back** of this book — so you've
got easy access to them while you're answering the questions.

Note: this book contains six Shakespeare Papers — three on scenes from Romeo and Juliet and three on scenes from The Tempest. The National Curriculum doesn't specify which Shakespeare plays you have to study at KS3, so these might not be the plays you're studying in class. It's best to check with your teacher if you're not sure.

To Get the Best Marks You Need to Keep Practising

1) These practice papers won't make you better at Maths, Science or even English,
    but they will show you what you **can** do, and what you **can't do**.

2) Do a test, **mark it** and look at what you got **wrong**. **That's** the stuff you need to **work on**.

3) **Go away**, **learn** those tricky bits, then **do the same test again**. If you're **still** getting questions
    wrong, you'll have to do even **more practice** and **test yourself again**.
    Keep going until you get the **best possible marks**.

4) It doesn't sound like a lot of **fun**, but it really will **help**.

Seven Top Tips for Doing Well

1) Read everything properly

The most important thing is to **understand** the questions.
Read everything **carefully** to be sure you're doing what they want.
In the **English Reading paper**, if you don't read the passages properly you can't
possibly get good marks. You've got to pay attention to **every single word**.

2) Follow all the instructions

Some questions have special instructions.

For example, in **Maths**, this pencil means "**WRITE YOUR ANSWER HERE**".
So make sure you do.

In the **English** questions you get a list of things to think about — include them **all**
in your answer. You'll get **more marks** if you do.

3) Look at the marks available

The **number of marks** you can get for a question gives you an idea of **how long** you
should spend on that question — spend **more time** on questions worth **more marks**.

4) Write your answers as clearly as you can

In a real exam, whoever's marking your paper won't be able to give you a mark if they
can't read your answer — even if it's right. You need to pay **special attention** to how
you write your answers in the **English** papers:

- **Plan** your answer carefully for the **Writing Paper** longer task. You don't really have
  time for big mistakes, and it's **clear**, **well-organised** writing that gets the best marks.

- Be especially careful about your **punctuation** and **spelling** on the writing questions.
  There are marks put aside for spelling in the shorter writing question.

5) Show your working

Make sure you write down your working whenever you do a calculation in the
Maths papers. Even if you get the answer **wrong**, you could get a mark for trying to
do the question in the **right way**. Questions which award marks for working have a
pencil marking the space where you should **clearly show your working**.

6) Check your work

Don't throw away easy marks — even if a question looks dead simple, you have to
check your answer and make sure it's sensible.

7) Use spare paper

If you're going to do the practice papers more than once, write your
answers on a separate bit of paper.

Recording Your Progress

You can use the tables below and on the next page to keep a **record** of **how well you do** in each test. Don't forget to **look back** at what you got **wrong**, so you know what to **practise** for the **next test**.

Stick Your Maths Marks in Here:

		Paper A (out of 60)	Paper B (out of 60)	Total Score (out of 120)
Set 1	First go			
	Second go			
	Third go			
Set 2	First go			
	Second go			
	Third go			
Set 3	First go			
	Second go			
	Third go			

Stick Your Science Marks in Here:

		Paper A (out of 75)	Paper B (out of 75)	Total Score (out of 150)
Set 1	First go			
	Second go			
	Third go			
Set 2	First go			
	Second go			
	Third go			
Set 3	First go			
	Second go			
	Third go			

Stick Your English Marks in Here:

		Reading Paper (out of 32)	Writing Paper (out of 50)	Shakespeare Paper (out of 18)	Total Score (out of 100)
Set A	First go				
	Second go				
	Third go				
Set B	First go				
	Second go				
	Third go				
Set C	First go				
	Second go				
	Third go				

Levels

As of **September 2014**, there are no KS3 assessment levels. But you can use the tables below to see what grades you'd have been likely to get under the **old levelling system**.

You'll need to use your **total score** for each subject.

Maths:

Mark	120-105	104-64	63-42	41-30	under 30
Level	8	7	6	5	N

Science:

Mark	150-105	104-73	72-42	41-36	under 36
Level	7	6	5	4	N

English:

Mark	100-68	67-51	50-30	29-17	under 17
Level	7	6	5	4	N

Key Stage 3

Mathematics Test

Practice Paper 1A
Calculator NOT allowed

Maths
KEY STAGE
3
PRACTICE PAPER
1A

Read this page, but don't open the booklet until your teacher says you can start. Write your name and school in the spaces below.

First Name _Ronan_

Last Name _Powell_

School _SHSS_

Remember

- The test is one hour long.

- Make sure you have these things with you before you start:
pen, pencil, rubber, ruler, angle measurer or protractor
and pair of compasses.
You may use tracing paper.

- There are some formulas you might need on page 6.

- The easier questions are at the start of the test.

- Try to answer all of the questions.

- Don't use any rough paper — write all your answers and
working in this test paper.

- Check your work carefully before the end of the test.

- If you're not sure what to do, ask your teacher.

Instructions

 This means write down your answer or show your working and your answer.

 You may not use a calculator in this test.

Formulas

Trapezium

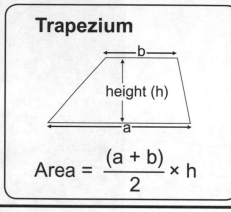

b

height (h)

a

Area = $\dfrac{(a + b)}{2} \times h$

Prism

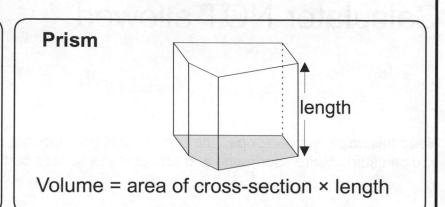

length

Volume = area of cross-section × length

---

1. ABCD is a rhombus. Angle A is 53°.

A   B

53°

D   C

(DIAGRAM NOT
TO SCALE)

(a) Write down the size of angle C.

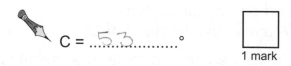 C = ...53..........°

1 mark

(b) Work out the size of angle B.

$360 - (53° \cdot 2) \div 2$

$= 360 - 106 \div 2$

$= 254 \div 2$

$= 127$

B = ...127..........°

2 marks

---

2. Complete the following statements.

(a) 700 cm³ = ...7000.... millilitres = ...7........ litres

(b) 63000 grams = ...63........ kilograms = ...0.63.... tonnes

3. Enlarge the shape below by a scale factor of ½, about centre of enlargement (0,0).

Maths — Practice Paper 1A

4. 120 Year 9 students were being taken on a school trip.
They could choose between a day at a theme park or the seaside.

41 boys wanted to go to the theme park.

14 girls wanted to go to the seaside.

56 of the students were girls.

Complete the table to show where the students decided to go.

	Theme Park	Seaside	Total
Boys	41	23	64
Girls	42	14	56
Total	83	37	120

2 marks

120 - 56 = 64 boys
56 girls

5. Gazza and Julia have each cut a rectangle out of paper.

One side is 10 cm.
The other side is n cm.

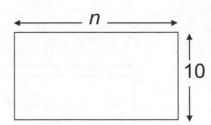

(a) They write down expressions for the perimeter of the rectangle.

Julia writes $2n + 20$

Gazza writes $2(n + 10)$

Put a circle around the correct statement below.

Julia is correct and Gazza is wrong.

Julia is wrong and Gazza is correct.

(Both Julia and Gazza are correct.)

Both Julia and Gazza are wrong.

1 mark

(b) Gazza cuts his rectangle in half.
He puts the halves side by side.

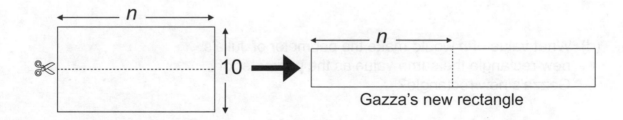

Gazza's new rectangle

What is the perimeter of Gazza's new rectangle?
Write your expression out as simply as possible.

 $2(n+10)$
2

$P = 4n + 10$ ....

2 marks

Continued over the page

(c) Julia cuts her rectangle in half a different way.
She puts them together to form a new rectangle.

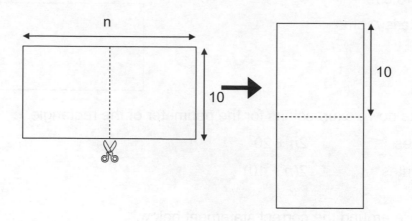

What is the perimeter of Julia's new rectangle?
Write your expression as simply as possible.

$P = 2n + 40$ ....

2 marks

(d) What value of n would make the perimeter of Julia's
new rectangle the same value as the perimeter of
Gazza's new rectangle?

$2n + 40 = 4n + 10$
$\quad -10 \qquad\qquad -10$

$2n + 30 = 4n$ $n = 15$ ....
$-2n \qquad\quad -2n$

1 mark

$\dfrac{30}{2} = \dfrac{2n}{2}$

$15 = n$

6. The diagram below shows a multiplication cross.

Opposite squares multiply together to give the answer in the middle square.

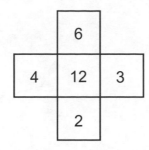

Complete the multiplication crosses below.

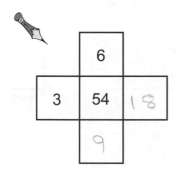

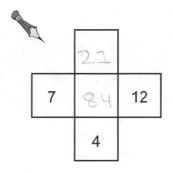

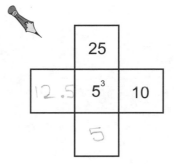

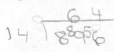

4 marks

7. Eleanor pays 14p per minute for a phone call to Morocco.

The total cost of the phone call is £8.96. (× 100)

Work out the length of the call in minutes.

..........64.......... minutes

2 marks

8. Solve these equations:

(a) $\dfrac{3x}{9} = -2$

$\times 9 \qquad \times 9$

$\dfrac{13x}{13} = \dfrac{-18}{3}$

$x = -6$

x = ...−6........

(b) $2y - 6 = 24$

$2y - 6 + 6 = 24 + 6$

$\dfrac{12y}{12} = \dfrac{30}{2}$

$y = 15$

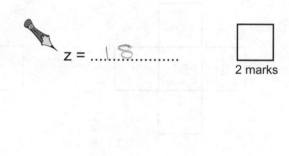

y = ...15..........

(c) $3z - 7 = 29 + z$

$+7$

$3z = 29 + z + 7$

$3z = 36 + z$

$-z \qquad -z$

$\dfrac{12z}{12} = \dfrac{36}{2}$

$z = 18$

z = ...18.........

9. A survey was conducted to find out how many people were registered with a National Health Service dentist, a private dentist or no dentist.

The pie chart shows the results.

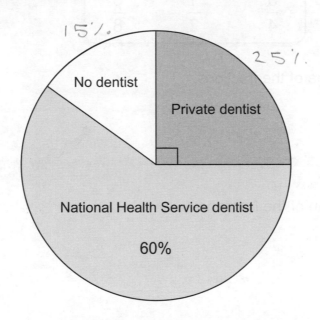

15%

25%

No dentist

Private dentist

National Health Service dentist

60%

(a) The angle on the pie chart for the people registered with a private dentist is 90°. What percentage of the people is this?

3.61%

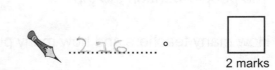 .....25.........%

☐ 1 mark

(b) Work out the angle on the pie chart for the people registered with a National Health Service dentist.

.....216.......° ☐ 2 marks

(c) 300 people were not registered with a dentist.
Work out how many people took part in the survey.

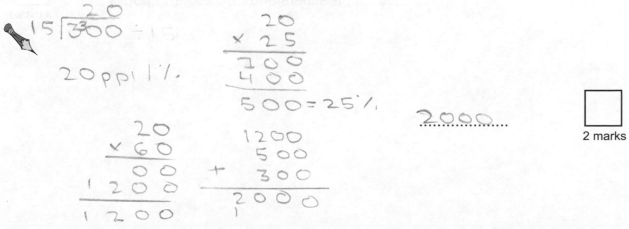

```
      20
 15 ⟌ 300  ÷ 15
   20 ppl 1%.

      20
    × 25
    ─────
    100
    400
    ─────
    500 = 25%

      20              1200
    × 60               500
    ─────          +   300
     00             ─────
  1 2 00             2000
  ─────               1
  1 200
```

2000

☐ 2 marks

10. Look at these fractions:

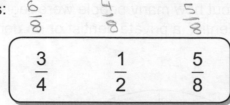

$$\frac{3}{4} \qquad \frac{1}{2} \qquad \frac{5}{8}$$

(a) Work out the range of the fractions.

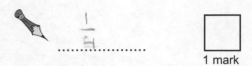

.... $\frac{1}{4}$

1 mark

(b) Work out the mean of the fractions.

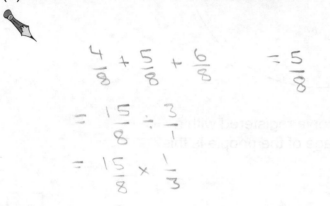

$$\frac{4}{8} + \frac{5}{8} + \frac{6}{8} \qquad = \frac{5}{8}$$

$$= \frac{15}{8} \div \frac{3}{1}$$

$$= \frac{15}{8} \times \frac{1}{3}$$

$$= \frac{15}{24}$$

.... $\frac{5}{8}$

2 marks

11. On a school trip the ratio of teachers to pupils was 2 : 7.
108 people went on the trip.

How many teachers and how many pupils went on the trip?

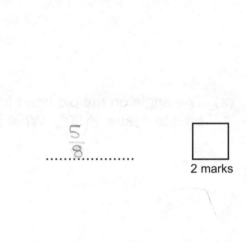

.........24......... teachers and ....84......... pupils

3 marks

$$\begin{array}{r} 1\ 2 \\ 9\,\overline{)1\,{}^{1}0\,{}^{0}8} \end{array}$$

$$2\cdot12 : 7\cdot12$$
$$24 : 84$$

$$\begin{array}{r} 24 \\ +\ 84 \\ \hline 1\ 0\ 8 \end{array}$$

12. In the year 2020, Josie will be x years old.

Her mum will be exactly four times Josie's age. 4x

Josie's Nanna is 30 years older than her Mum. 4x + 30

Josie's Nanna will be 78 years old in 2020.

(a) Use this information to form an algebraic expression and solve it to find x. You must show your working.

$(78 - 30) \div 4 = x$

$48 \div 4 = x$

$12 = x$

x = ...12...........

2 marks

(b) In what year was Josie born?

2008

1 mark

13. Here is the graph of the straight line y = -2x + 3.

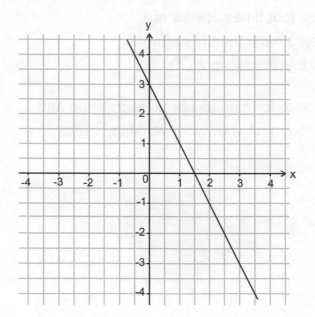

(a) A point on the line y = -2x + 3 has an x-coordinate of 25.

What is the y-coordinate of the point?

$y = -2(25) + 3$

$y = -50 + 3$

$y = -47$

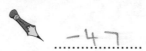 ....-47..........

☐ 1 mark

(b) A point on the line y = -2x + 3 has a y-coordinate of -31.

What is the x-coordinate of the point?

$-31 = -2x + 3$ $17 = x$

$-31 - 3 = -2x + 3 - 3$

$\dfrac{-34}{-2} = \dfrac{-2x}{-2}$

 ....17..........

☐ 1 mark

(c) Using an algebraic method, find the point that lies on both
the straight lines y = -2x + 3 and y = 6x – 17.

You must show your working.

(.........., ...)

☐ 3 marks

14. A bag of 50 mixed nuts contains almonds, peanuts and cashew nuts.

I randomly select a nut from the bag.

The probability of selecting a peanut is 0.42 and the probability of selecting an almond is 0.26.

(a) What is the probability of selecting an almond or a peanut?

....

1 mark

(b) What is the probability of selecting a cashew nut?

....

1 mark

(c) How many peanuts are in the bag?

....

1 mark

15. In a school 75% of the pupils have fillings.

20% of the pupils with fillings also have braces.

Work out the percentage of pupils in the school with fillings and braces.

...........................%

3 marks

16. (a) Rearrange the equation 2d + 6 = e to make d the subject.

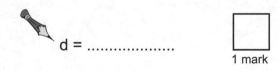 d = ...

1 mark

(b) Rearrange the equation $8 + 5f^2 = 3g$ to make f the subject.

 f = ...

2 marks

17. You have these numbers:

| 0.1 | 3 | 20 | 0.2 | 0.03 | 1 |

(a)   Choose the two numbers which give the lowest answer.
        Fill in the blanks and work out the answer.

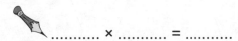 .... × .... = ...

(b)   Which two numbers give the answer 200?

 .... ÷ .... = 200

(c)   Look at these expressions.

$$p - 3 \qquad 2p \qquad p^2 \qquad \frac{2}{p} \qquad \frac{p}{2}$$

Which gives the greatest value when p is between 0 and 1?

 ....

18. These two kites are similar:

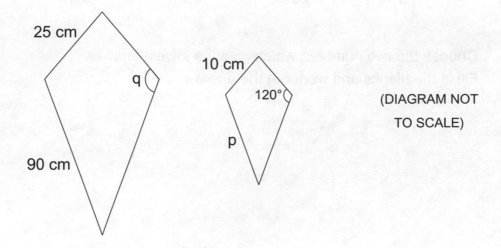

25 cm

q

10 cm

120°

90 cm

p

(DIAGRAM NOT TO SCALE)

(a) Work out the length of side p in the smaller kite.

p = ... cm

2 marks

(b) What is the size of angle q in the larger kite?

q = ... °

1 mark

END OF TEST

Key Stage 3

Mathematics Test

Practice Paper 1B

Calculator allowed

Read this page, but don't open the booklet until your teacher says you can start. Write your name and school in the spaces below.

First Name _____

Last Name _____

School _____

Remember

- The test is one hour long.

- Make sure you have these things with you before you start: pen, pencil, rubber, ruler, calculator, angle measurer or protractor and pair of compasses.
  You may use tracing paper.

- There are some formulas you might need on page 22.

- The easier questions are at the start of the test.

- Try to answer all of the questions.

- Don't use any rough paper — write all your answers and working in this test paper.

- Check your work carefully before the end of the test.

- If you're not sure what to do, ask your teacher.

Instructions

This means write down your answer or show your working and your answer.

You may use a calculator in this test.

Formulas

Trapezium

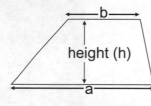

Area = $\dfrac{(a + b)}{2} \times h$

Prism

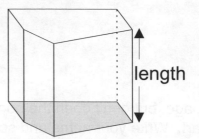

length

Volume = area of cross-section × length

---

1. (a) Use your calculator to find the answer to $\sqrt{15200} \div 3.2^4$.

Write down the full answer displayed on your calculator.

 ....

☐ 1 mark

(b) Round your answer to part (a) to three decimal places.

 ....

☐ 1 mark

(c) Use your calculator to find the answer to

$\dfrac{151 - 39}{90 - 55} =$ ....

☐ 1 mark

---

2. (a) Shade in four tenths of this shape:

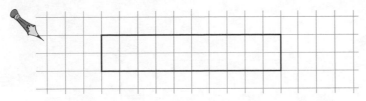

1 mark

(b) What proportion of this shape is shaded?
Give your answer as a decimal number.

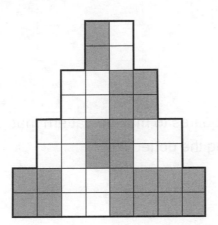

....

1 mark

(c) What percentage of this diagram is shaded?

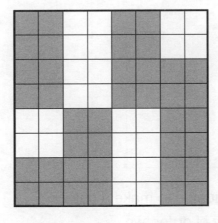

.... %

1 mark

3. (a) This diagram has four small squares shaded in.

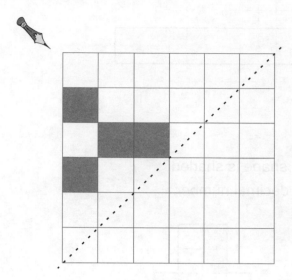

Shade in four more small squares to make a pattern that
has a line of symmetry along the dotted line.

(b) Here is another diagram with four small squares shaded in.

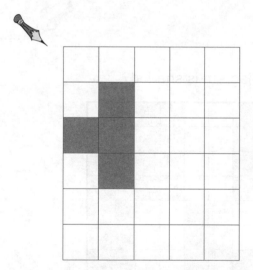

Shade in four more small squares to make a pattern
that has rotational symmetry of order two.

4. This table shows the number of students in a school who are learning to play a musical instrument:

	Boys	Girls
Guitar	15	3
Clarinet	2	11
Keyboard	4	5

A student is chosen at random.

(a) Find the probability that the student chosen will be a boy.

1 mark

(b) Find the probability that the student chosen will play the keyboard.

1 mark

(c) A guitarist is chosen at random.
Find the probability that the guitarist is a girl.

1 mark

5. Shops A and B both sell cans of cola.

Cola only 36p per can

Shop A

SPECIAL DEAL
Pack of 6 cans of Cola

only £2.19

Shop B

(a) How much does it cost to buy 8 cans of Cola from shop A?

£ ....

1 mark

(b) Abigail wants to buy 18 cans of Cola.
Which shop would be cheaper and by how much?
You must show your working.

Shop .... by £ ....

2 marks

6. Mr Smith is on a diet. He weighs 105 kg. His target weight is 77 kg.

If he loses 1.4 kg each week, how many weeks will it take him to reach his target weight?

.... weeks

2 marks

7. Simplify these expressions:

(a) $6 - 3s + 5s - 2$

.... ☐ 1 mark

(b) $9t^2 + 3t + 2t^2$

.... ☐ 1 mark

(c) $6u \times 3u$

.... ☐ 1 mark

(d) $\dfrac{16v^3}{4v}$

.... ☐ 1 mark

8. The table shows the speed in miles per hour of a tennis player's serve during a match.

Speed (s) in mph	frequency (f)	midpoint (x)	fx
90 < s ≤ 100	12	95	1140
100 < s ≤ 110	18	....	....
110 < s ≤ 120	28	....	....
120 < s ≤ 130	7	....	....
Total	65	-	7125

(a) Complete the table.

2 marks

(b) Work out an estimate of the mean speed of the tennis player's serve.

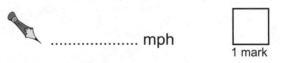 .... mph

1 mark

9. The diagram shows the trapezium ABCD.

Angle A measures 130° and angles B and C are both right angles.

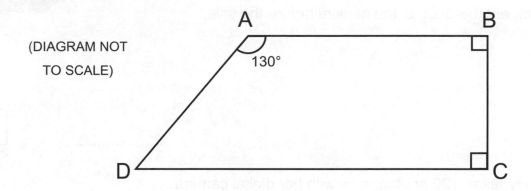

(DIAGRAM NOT TO SCALE)

The trapezium is cut into two shapes labelled P and Q.

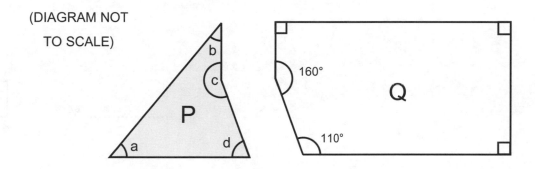

(DIAGRAM NOT TO SCALE)

Work out the sizes of angles a, b, c and d.

angle a = ... °

angle b = ... °

angle c = ... °

angle d = ... °

4 marks

10. In a sale, the price of a digital camera is reduced by 18%.
The new price of the camera is £287.

(a) Work out the price of the camera before the sale.

£...................

(b) Jenny takes 120 photographs with her digital camera.
She prints off 54 photographs and discards the rest.

Work out the percentage of the photographs that are discarded.

.... %

11. A glass tumbler is a cylinder with a radius of 3 cm and a height of 12 cm.

(DIAGRAM NOT
TO SCALE)

Calculate the volume of the glass tumbler.

.... cm³

12.

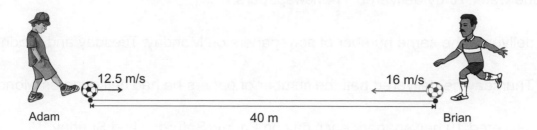

12.5 m/s   16 m/s

Adam   40 m   Brian

Adam and Brian are standing 40 metres apart.

Adam kicks a ball to Brian at an average speed of 12.5 m/s.

Brian kicks the ball back to Adam at an average speed of 16 m/s.

Work out the total time, in seconds, that the ball takes to travel from
Adam to Brian and back again.

.... seconds

2 marks

13. In one week, Andy delivered 114 newspapers.

He delivered the same number of newspapers on Monday, Tuesday and Wednesday.

On Thursday he delivered half the number of papers he had delivered on Monday.

He delivered 10 newspapers each day on Friday, Saturday and Sunday.

How many newspapers did he deliver on Tuesday?

....

3 marks

14. Multiply out the brackets in this expression.
Write your answer as simply as possible.

(x + 7)(x − 4)

....

2 marks

15. The points P and Q lie on a straight-line graph, as shown below.

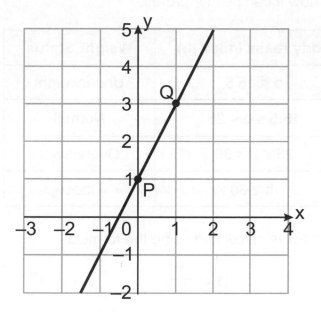

(a) Write down the coordinates of P and Q.

 P is (............ , ...) and Q is (............ , ...)

1 mark

(b) Show that the gradient of the line PQ is 2.

2 marks

(c) Write down the equation of the line that points P and Q lie on.

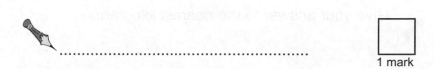 ....

1 mark

Maths — Practice Paper 1B

16. Body mass index is a number used to identify possible weight problems in adults. The table below shows how it can be interpreted.

Body mass index (b)	Weight Status
b < 18.5	Underweight
18.5 ≤ b < 25	Normal
25 ≤ b < 30	Overweight
b ≥ 30	Obese

A person's body mass index is calculated using the formula

$$b = \frac{w}{h^2}$$

where **b** = body mass index, **w** = weight in kg and **h** = height in metres.

(a) Adam weighs 70 kilograms and is 1.75 metres tall.
Work out his body mass index and find his weight status.

Body mass index = ...   Weight status = ...

2 marks

(b) Jodie has a body mass index of 19 and weighs 55 kilograms.
Work out how tall she is. Give your answer correct to 2 decimal places.

.... m

2 marks

(c) Daniel is 1.64 metres tall and has a body mass index of 28.
How much weight must he lose to achieve a body mass index of 24?
Give your answer to the nearest kilogram.

.... kg

3 marks

17. The diagram shows the cross-section of a dry ski slope.

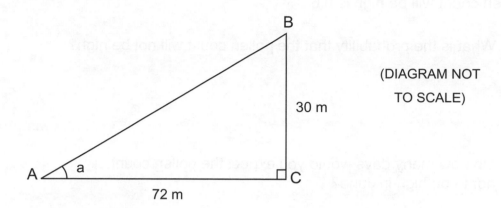

(DIAGRAM NOT TO SCALE)

The ski slope AB stands on horizontal ground AC of length 72 m.
The height of the ski slope is 30 m.

(a) Work out the length of the ski slope AB.

.... m

2 marks

(b) The ski slope makes an angle of a° with the horizontal.
Work out the size of angle a. Give your answer correct to 1 decimal place.

.... °

2 marks

18. On any given day in June, the probability that the
pollen count will be high is 0.6.

(a) What is the probability that the pollen count will not be high?

....

1 mark

(b) On how many days would you expect the pollen count
not to be high in June?

....

1 mark

(c) Find the probability that the pollen count will be high on each
of the first three days in June.

....

1 mark

END OF TEST

Key Stage 3

Mathematics Test

Practice Paper 2A
Calculator NOT allowed

Maths

KEY STAGE
3

PRACTICE PAPER
2A

Read this page, but don't open the booklet until your teacher says you can start. Write your name and school in the spaces below.

First Name _____

Last Name _____

School _____

Remember

☐ The test is one hour long.

☐ Make sure you have these things with you before you start: pen, pencil, rubber, ruler, angle measurer or protractor and pair of compasses.
You may use tracing paper.

☐ There are some formulas you might need on page 38.

☐ The easier questions are at the start of the test.

☐ Try to answer all of the questions.

☐ Don't use any rough paper — write all your answers and working in this test paper.

☐ Check your work carefully before the end of the test.

☐ If you're not sure what to do, ask your teacher.

Instructions

This means write down your answer or show your working and your answer.

You may not use a calculator in this test.

Formulas

Trapezium

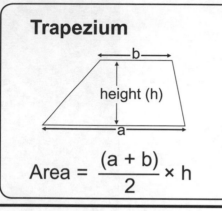

$$\text{Area} = \frac{(a + b)}{2} \times h$$

Prism

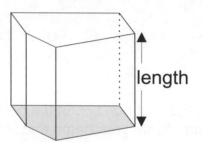

Volume = area of cross-section × length

1. A bag of fruit sweets contains 5 strawberry flavour, 4 raspberry flavour and 6 blackberry flavour.

   Debbie chooses a sweet at random. Find the probability that it is:

   (a) raspberry flavour

    ....

   1 mark

   (b) not blackberry flavour

    ....

   1 mark

   (c) Steve has another bag of fruit sweets. Half of them are strawberry flavour.
   Tick the correct box to show who has the most strawberry sweets.

   ☐ Debbie   ☐ Steve   ☐ Cannot tell

   Explain your answer.

   1 mark

2. (a) Construct this triangle accurately in the space below.

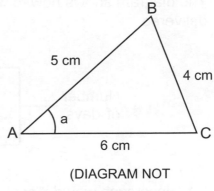

5 cm

4 cm

a

A

6 cm

C

B

(DIAGRAM NOT TO SCALE)

3 marks

(b) Measure the size of angle a.

a = ...°

1 mark

3. Mr. Wardell ordered 52 calculators for the Maths department.
Each calculator cost £2.32.

Estimate how much Mr. Wardell spent on calculators.

£....................

2 marks

4. The diagram shows how to work out the cost of hiring a cement mixer and having it delivered.

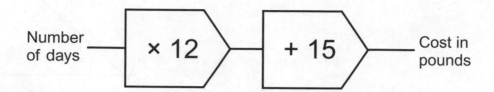

Number of days —— [× 12] —— [+ 15] —— Cost in pounds

(a) How much would it cost to hire the cement mixer for 7 days?

£....................

1 mark

(b) Marlon paid £147.

How many days did he have the cement mixer for?

....

2 marks

(c) The 12 in the diagram above represents the daily charge for hiring the cement mixer.

What does the 15 represent?

....

1 mark

5. Solve the following equations:

(a) $3x + 7 = 25$

x = ...

1 mark

(b) $4(x - 2) = 30$

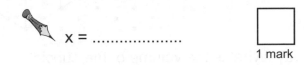

x = ...

1 mark

(c) $2x - 9 = 5x + 3$

x = ...

1 mark

6. Fill in the gaps to complete these calculations correctly:

(a) $7 + \text{...........} = 2$

1 mark

(b) $5 - \text{...........} = 8$

1 mark

(c) $-2 \times \text{...........} = -8$

1 mark

(d) $\text{...........} \div -4 = -3$

1 mark

7. The cuboid below is made of 2 cm cubes.

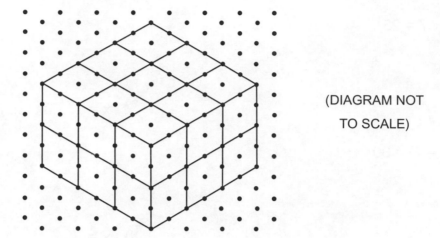

(DIAGRAM NOT
TO SCALE)

(a) What is the volume of the cuboid?

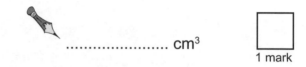

.... cm³

1 mark

(b) What is the surface area of the cuboid?

.... cm²

2 marks

(c) The diagram shows a 2 cm cube. Add more 2 cm cubes
to form a cuboid with a volume of 48 cm³.

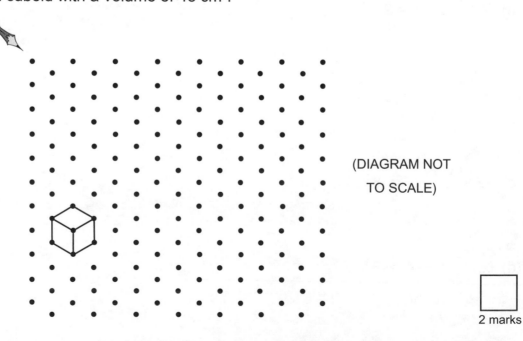

(DIAGRAM NOT
TO SCALE)

2 marks

8. Roop was studying the birds at a wildlife sanctuary.
She noticed that the ratio of ducks to geese to swans was 3 : 5 : 2.

(a) What percentage of the birds were swans?

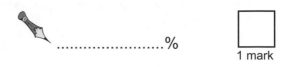

.........................%

(b) She counted 18 ducks. How many geese and swans were there?

.... geese

.... swans

9. Write the following values in order of size, starting with the smallest.

0.3 $\frac{1}{2}$ $\frac{2}{5}$ 0.2

....

3 marks

10. Here are six sequences and six expressions.

Match each sequence with the correct expression for its nth term.
The first one has been done for you.

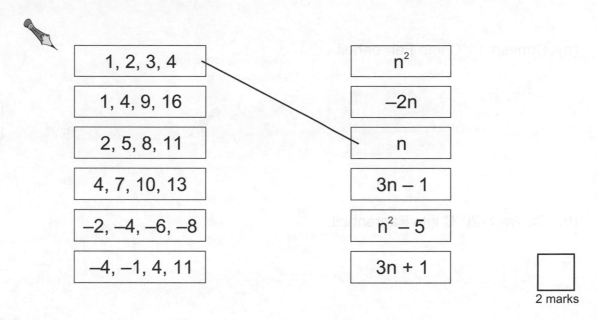

2 marks

11. The formula for converting temperature in Celsius (C) to Fahrenheit (F) is

$$F = \frac{9C}{5} + 32$$

(a) Convert 10°C into Fahrenheit.

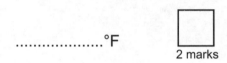 ....°F

1 mark

(b) Convert -20°C into Fahrenheit.

....................°F

2 marks

(c) Rearrange the formula so that it can be used to convert Fahrenheit into Celsius.

C = ...

2 marks

12. Look at the triangle below.

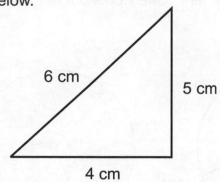

6 cm

5 cm

(DIAGRAM NOT
TO SCALE)

4 cm

Is this a right-angled triangle? Explain how you know.

2 marks

13. Expand and simplify the following expression.

$$(x + 5)(x + 4)$$

....

2 marks

14. Pat is playing a game with two spinners. She works out her score by multiplying the two numbers she spins together.

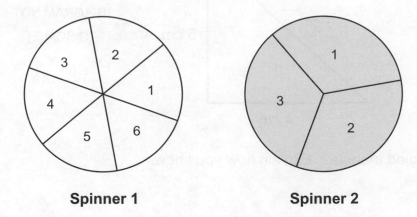

Spinner 1   Spinner 2

(a) Complete the table to show all her possible scores.

Spinner 1

	1	2	3	4	5	6
1	1	2	....	....	....	....
2	2	4	....	....	....	....
3	3	6	....	....	....	....

Spinner 2

2 marks

(b) Use your table to work out the probability that Pat's score is an odd number.

....   1 mark

15. The diagram shows an equilateral triangle ABC.

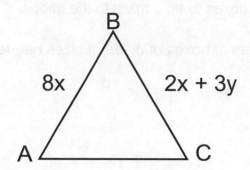

Side AB is of length 8x. Side BC is of length 2x + 3y.
The perimeter of the triangle is 36.

Use algebra to find the values of x and y.

x = ...

y = ...

3 marks

16. A cake machine produces 10 000 cakes at a time.
The cakes have to be put into boxes to take them to the shops.

(a) The table shows the numbers of boxes of different sizes needed
to hold all of these cakes.

Complete the table:

Number of cakes per box	100		500		2000	5000
Number of boxes		40	20	10		2

3 marks

(b) Write an equation using symbols to connect **T**, the number of cakes
made at a time, **B,** the capacity of a box and **N**, the number of boxes.

....

1 mark

(c) The factory gets a new machine which produces cakes
at a rate of 50 per minute.
How long does it now take to produce 10 000 cakes?

Show your working.

.... hours .... minutes

2 marks

17. The highest mountain in the world is Mount Everest.
Its height in feet is 2.903×10^4.

(a) Write 2.903×10^4 as an ordinary number.

....

(b) The highest mountain in the UK is Ben Nevis.
Its height in feet is 4.41×10^3.

How much higher is Mount Everest than Ben Nevis?
Give your answer in standard form.

.... feet

18. Find the value of y in each of the equations below.

(a) $6^y = 1$

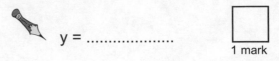 y = ...
☐ 1 mark

(b) $3^y = 81$

y = ...
☐ 1 mark

(c) $72 = y^3 \times 3^2$

y = ...
☐ 1 mark

END OF TEST

Key Stage 3

Mathematics Test

Practice Paper 2B

Calculator allowed

Read this page, but don't open the booklet until your teacher says you can start. Write your name and school in the spaces below.

First Name _____

Last Name _____

School _____

Remember

- The test is one hour long.

- Make sure you have these things with you before you start: pen, pencil, rubber, ruler, calculator, angle measurer or protractor and pair of compasses.
  You may use tracing paper.

- There are some formulas you might need on page 54.

- The easier questions are at the start of the test.

- Try to answer all of the questions.

- Don't use any rough paper — write all your answers and working in this test paper.

- Check your work carefully before the end of the test.

- If you're not sure what to do, ask your teacher.

Maths

KEY STAGE
3

PRACTICE PAPER
2B

Instructions

 This means write down your answer or show your working and your answer.

 You may use a calculator in this test.

Formulas

Trapezium

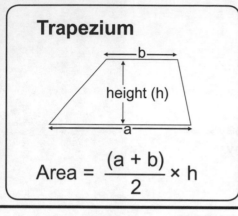

Area = $\dfrac{(a + b)}{2} \times h$

Prism

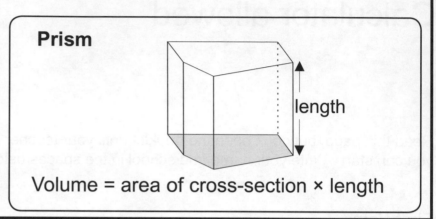

Volume = area of cross-section × length

1.   The diagram shows two flags and a straight line.

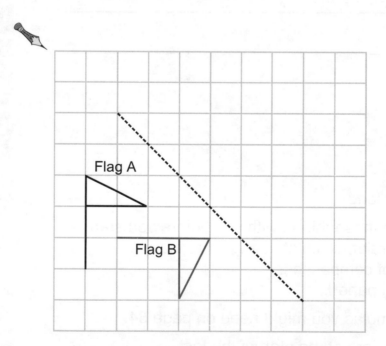

(a) Flag A has been rotated 90° clockwise to give Flag B.
     Mark the centre of rotation with a cross.

1 mark

(b) Flag B is reflected in the straight line. Draw its new position.

1 mark

2. Jeff wants to buy a bottle of water from a vending machine.
The bottle costs 45p. Jeff only has 5p, 10p and 20p coins.

Complete the table to show all the ways he can pay exactly 45p.

Number of 5p coins	Number of 10p coins	Number of 20p coins
1	0	2
....	....	....
....	....	....
....	....	....
....	....	....
....	....	....
....	....	....
....	....	....
....	....	....

3 marks

3. (a) Shade $\frac{4}{7}$ of this shape:

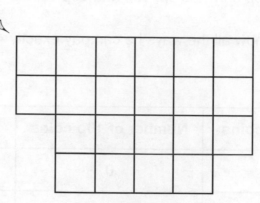

1 mark

(b) Shade 0.3 of this shape:

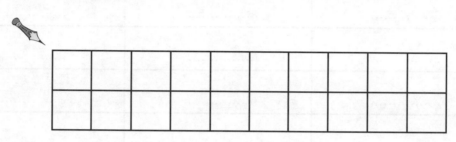

1 mark

(c) Shade 45% of this shape:

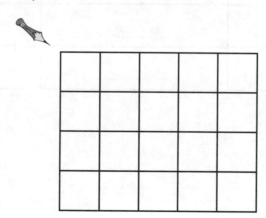

1 mark

4. Peter timed how long it took him to do his last five sets of Maths homework.

Set	Time to do homework (minutes)
1	17
2	26
3	52
4	31
5	43

(a) What is the range of the times taken?

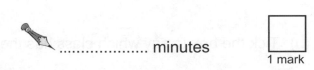 .... minutes

(b) What was the median time taken?

.... minutes

(c) Pattie timed how long it took her to do the same five sets of homework.

The range of her times was 20 minutes.
The median of her times was 25 minutes.

Write down a set of times that Pattie might have taken.

5. Helen drew two pie charts to show what pets are owned by students in classes 9A and 9B.

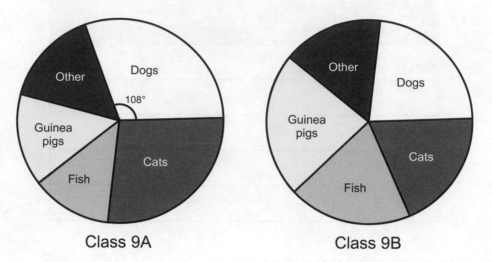

Class 9A   Class 9B

(a) In class 9A, the section for dogs represents 9 students.

How many students are in class 9A?

....

2 marks

(b) Tick the box to say which class has the most dog owners.

☐   ☐   ☐

9A   9B   Cannot tell

Explain your answer.

1 mark

6. (a) Write down three pairs of coordinates that fit the rule **x + y = 7**.

(.........., ...), (.........., ...), (.........., ...)

2 marks

(b) Draw the graph of x + y = 7 on the grid below.

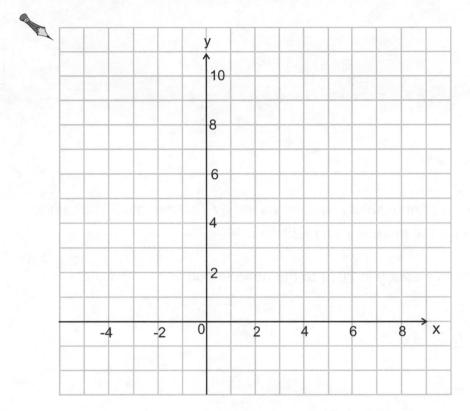

2 marks

7. The diagram shows part of Bekani's garden.

The crosses represent the positions of two trees.

He wants to lay a path so that it is equidistant from the two trees.

Construct the locus that the path should take.

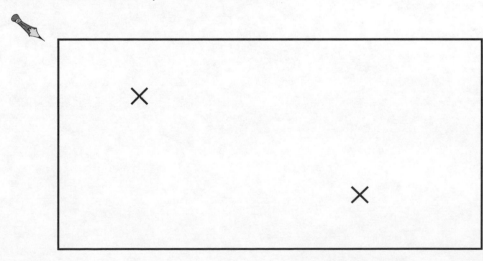

2 marks

8. In 2012 Gail's annual salary was £32 200.
   In 2013 her salary was increased to £35 800.

   (a) What was the percentage increase in her salary?

   ....%

   2 marks

   (b) In 2013 Mark's annual salary was increased by 7% from his 2012 salary.
   His salary after the increase was £28 400.

   What was Mark's salary in 2012 to the nearest pound?

   £....................

   2 marks

9. Miss Singleton asked her Year 9 form group how much time they had spent watching television over the weekend.

The answers are shown in the graph below.

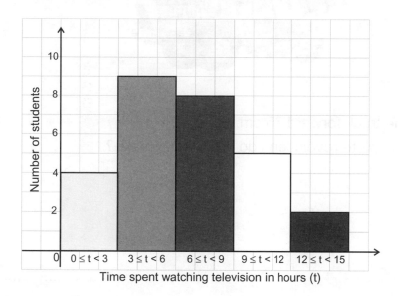

(a) How many students did she ask?

....

(b) Calculate an estimate of the mean time spent watching television.
Give your answer in hours and minutes to the nearest 10 minutes.

.... hours and .... minutes

10. The wheels on Dominic's toy truck have a diameter of 2 cm.

(a) He pushes the truck forward 65 cm.
How many complete revolutions do the wheels make?

....

2 marks

(b) What is the area of the cross section of a wheel on the truck?

.... cm²

2 marks

The toy is a scale model of a real truck.

The cross sectional area of a wheel on the real truck is 0.58 m².

(c) Find the scale factor of the enlargement that would transform
the toy truck into a truck the same size as the real truck.

....

3 marks

11. The diagram shows part of the edge of a regular polygon.

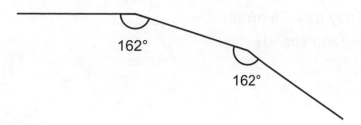

162°

162°

(a) What size are the exterior angles of the polygon?

.... °

1 mark

(b) How many sides does the polygon have?

....

1 mark

12. Louise travels 18 miles to work.

(a) One day the journey took 35 minutes.
What was her average speed?

.... mph

(b) If she drove at an average speed of 38 miles per hour,
how long would it take her to get to work?

.... minutes

(c) Clarissa took 25 minutes to drive to work.
Her average speed during the journey was 40 miles per hour.
How long was her journey?

.... miles

13. Find the missing side x in each of the following right-angled triangles.

(a)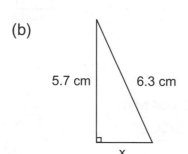

3.4 cm

x

7.3 cm

(DIAGRAM NOT
TO SCALE)

x = ... cm

2 marks

(b)

5.7 cm   6.3 cm

x

(DIAGRAM NOT
TO SCALE)

x = ... cm

2 marks

14. The formula for the volume, V, of a sphere of radius r is $V = \frac{4}{3}\pi r^3$.

(a) Find the volume of a sphere with radius 3.6 cm.

.... cm³

2 marks

(b) Find the radius of a sphere with a volume of 28.3 cm³.

.... cm

2 marks

15. (a) Find the size of angle a in the right-angled triangle below.

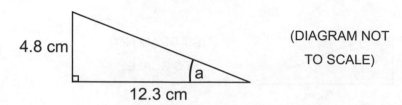

(DIAGRAM NOT
TO SCALE)

a = ...°

2 marks

(b) Find the length of side b in this right-angled triangle:

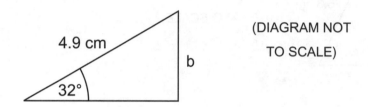

(DIAGRAM NOT
TO SCALE)

b = ... cm

2 marks

16. The Clewes family and the Bleach family visited the Italian Gardens.

The Clewes family consisted of 3 adults and 2 children and they were charged £31.

The Bleach family consisted of 2 adults and 5 children and they were charged £39.

(a) Using **a** to represent the adult cost and **c** to represent the child cost, write down 2 equations.

2 marks

(b) Solve your equations to find the cost of entry for adults and children.
You must show an algebraic method.

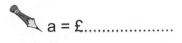 a = £....................

c = £....................

2 marks

17. The diagram shows three similar rectangles — A, B and C.

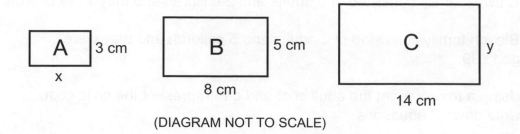

(DIAGRAM NOT TO SCALE)

(a) Find the missing lengths x and y.

x = ... cm

y = ... cm

2 marks

(b) What is the scale factor of the enlargement that
would transform C to A?

....

1 mark

END OF TEST

Key Stage 3

Mathematics Test

Practice Paper 3A
Calculator NOT allowed

Maths

KEY STAGE
3

PRACTICE PAPER
3A

Read this page, but don't open the booklet until your teacher says you can start. Write your name and school in the spaces below.

First Name _____

Last Name _____

School _____

Remember

- The test is one hour long.

- Make sure you have these things with you before you start: pen, pencil, rubber, ruler, angle measurer or protractor and pair of compasses.
  You may use tracing paper.

- There are some formulas you might need on page 70.

- The easier questions are at the start of the test.

- Try to answer all of the questions.

- Don't use any rough paper — write all your answers and working in this test paper.

- Check your work carefully before the end of the test.

- If you're not sure what to do, ask your teacher.

Instructions

This means write down your answer or show your working and your answer.

You may not use a calculator in this test.

Formulas

Trapezium

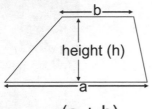

Area = $\dfrac{(a + b)}{2} \times h$

Prism

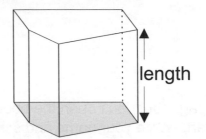

length

Volume = area of cross-section × length

---

1. (a) Show that 8 × 37 = 296.

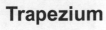

☐

1 mark

(b) What is 32 × 37? You can use part (a) to help you.

.... ☐

2 marks

2. David is d years old.

His younger sister Katya is k years old.

Their father is three times as old as David.

Write down expressions for each of the following:

(a) David's age in 10 years time.

.... 　1 mark

(b) Katya's age 7 years ago.

.... 　1 mark

(c) Their father's age.

.... 　1 mark

(d) The difference between their father's age and David's age.
Simplify your answer as much as possible.

.... 　1 mark

(e) David's age, when Katya is as old as he is now.
Simplify your answer as much as possible.

.... 　2 marks

3. A triangle has a base 20 cm long.

The area of the triangle is 100 cm².

height

Area = 100 cm²

(Not to scale)

20 cm

What is the perpendicular height of the triangle? Show your working.

.... cm

2 marks

4. (a) I am thinking of a number. My number is a multiple of 3.

Anish says: "Because 3 is an odd number, your number must be odd."

Is Anish correct? Explain your answer.

2 marks

(b) I am thinking of a different number. It is a multiple of 12.

Tick all the statements from the list below that must be true.

☐ It is greater than 12

☐ It is a multiple of 3

☐ It is divisible by 6

☐ It is not divisible by 11

☐ It is a factor of 24

2 marks

5. Look at this sequence of patterns made with crosses:

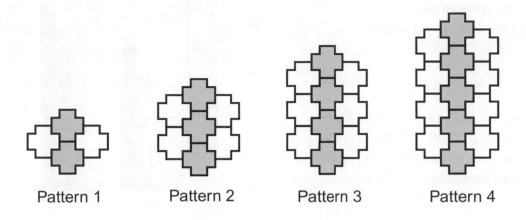

Pattern 1   Pattern 2   Pattern 3   Pattern 4

(a) How many grey crosses will there be in the 10th pattern?

....

1 mark

(b) How many white crosses will there be in the 10th pattern?

....

1 mark

(c) How many crosses will there be altogether in the 100th pattern?

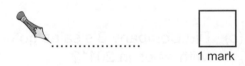

....

1 mark

6. Fill in the missing fraction in each of the sums below.

(a) $\dfrac{1}{7} + \dfrac{1}{5} =$

....

1 mark

(b) $\dfrac{2}{13} - \dfrac{2}{39} =$

....

1 mark

7. The bar graph shows the percentage increase in sales of books by two publishing companies, Company A and Company B.

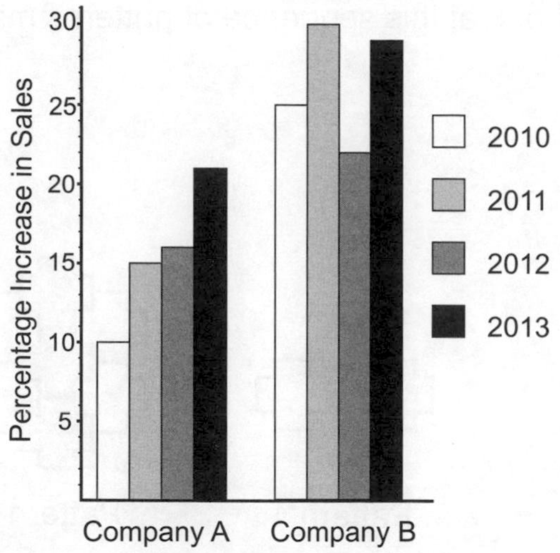

(a) In 2011 Company A's sales were 15% more than in the previous year.

By what percentage did Company B increase its sales in 2011?

Percentage increase in sales = ... %

1 mark

(b) The bars for Company B are all taller than the bars for Company A.
Does this mean that Company B had higher sales than Company A?

☐ Yes   ☐ No

Explain your answer.

1 mark

(c) Did Company B's sales go down in 2012 compared with sales in 2011?

☐ Yes   ☐ No

Explain your answer.

1 mark

8. The diagram shows two common sizes of paper, called A4 and A3.

A3 paper is an enlargement of A4 paper.

One A3 sheet is exactly the same size as two A4 sheets next to each other.

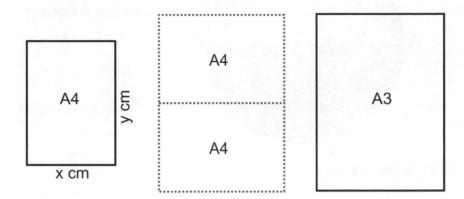

A4 paper is x cm wide and y cm long.

(a) Use the second diagram to write down the width and length of A3 paper.

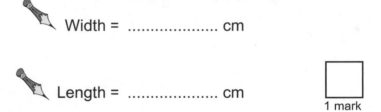

Width = ... cm

Length = ... cm

(b) Explain why $\dfrac{2x}{y} = \dfrac{y}{x}$.

(c) Sophie says "That means y = 2x". Sophie is not correct.
Write down a correct version of her statement.

y = ...

9. The diagram shows a circle with diameter AB, which contains the triangle ABC. The circle has an area of 4π cm².

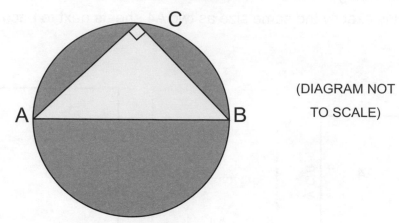

(DIAGRAM NOT TO SCALE)

(a) Find the radius of the circle.

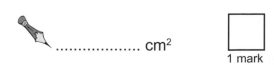

.... cm

1 mark

(b) The side BC of the right-angled triangle is $\sqrt{8}$ cm.
Show that the triangle is isosceles.

2 marks

(c) Find the area of the triangle.

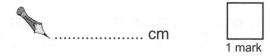

.... cm²

1 mark

10. At a party there are:

25 three-year olds

20 four-year olds

two mothers, aged 28 and 32

three fathers, aged 30, 31 and 33

one grandmother, aged 68

(a) Put the following in order, from smallest to largest.
(You do not need to do any calculations.)

mean age   **median age**   **modal age**

1. ....

2. ....

3. ....

1 mark

(b) Explain how you knew which was the largest without working it out.

1 mark

11. In my Gran's cupboard, she has tins of peaches, pineapple and pears.

The tins are either large or small.

The table shows the numbers of each type of tin Gran has.

	Large tins	Small tins
Peaches	4	3
Pineapple	8	4
Pears	2	3

(a) Gran chooses a tin at random.

What is the probability it is a small tin of pears?

....

1 mark

(b) My younger sister takes the labels off all of the tins.
Gran wants a tin of peaches.

Which size tin should Gran open to have the best chance of getting a tin of peaches? Explain your answer, including any calculations.

3 marks

12. Look at the triangle below.

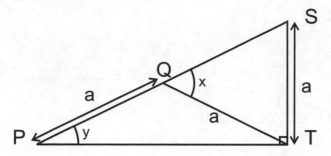

(DIAGRAM NOT TO SCALE)

(a) Explain carefully why x = 2y.

2 marks

(b) Find the value of y.

y = ...°

2 marks

13. (a) Calculate 10% of £200.

£................... ▢ 1 mark

(b) Use your answer to (a) to find 2½% of £200.

£................... ▢ 1 mark

(c) In Meanland, there is a tax of 22½% on every item that is sold.
A television costs £220 before tax.

Work out how much it costs including the tax.

£................... ▢ 2 marks

14. Tick the statements that are true.

(a)

☐ When x is even,
x(x + 3) is odd.

☐ When x is even,
x(x + 3) is even.

☐

1 mark

(b)

☐ When x is odd,
$x^2 + 1$ is even.

☐ When x is odd,
$x^2 + 1$ is odd.

☐

1 mark

(c)

☐ $x^2 + x$ is
always odd.

☐ $x^2 + x$ is
always even.

☐

1 mark

15. I have a list of five numbers.

The mean of the numbers is 4.

The mode of the numbers is 2.

The median of the numbers is 3.

Write down one possibility for my list of numbers.

☐

2 marks

16. (a) Find the area of the trapezium below.

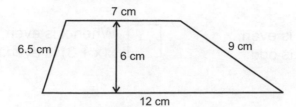

.... cm²

2 marks

(b) This prism has the trapezium from part (a) as its cross-section.

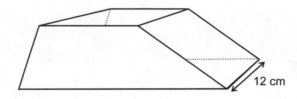

12 cm

Find its volume.

.... cm³

2 marks

17. In a science experiment, Sabiha investigated the relationship between temperature and time taken for a chemical reaction to finish.

She plotted a graph of her results.

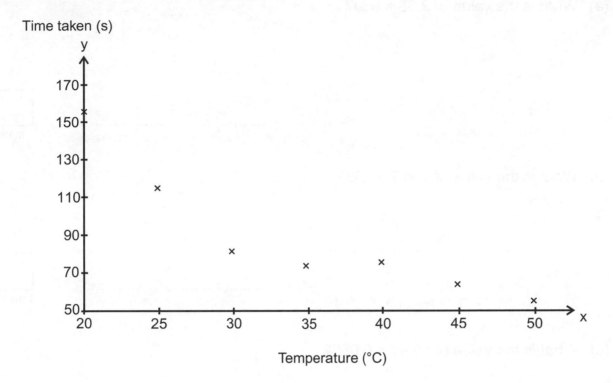

(a) What type of correlation does the graph show?

(b) Sabiha thought the equation of the line of best fit was y = 3x + 20.

Give two reasons why this cannot be correct.

18. Use the following calculation to answer the questions below.

$$23.8 \times 6.5 = 154.7$$

(a) What is the value of 2.38 × 650?

.... ☐

1 mark

(b) What is the value of 154.7 ÷ 238?

.... ☐

1 mark

(c) What is the value of 15.47 ÷ 0.065?

.... ☐

1 mark

END OF TEST

Key Stage 3

Mathematics Test

Practice Paper 3B

Calculator allowed

Maths

KEY STAGE
3

PRACTICE PAPER
3B

Read this page, but don't open the booklet until your teacher says you can start. Write your name and school in the spaces below.

First Name _____

Last Name _____

School _____

Remember

- The test is one hour long.

- Make sure you have these things with you before you start: pen, pencil, rubber, ruler, calculator, angle measurer or protractor and pair of compasses.
  You may use tracing paper.

- There are some formulas you might need on page 86.

- The easier questions are at the start of the test.

- Try to answer all of the questions.

- Don't use any rough paper — write all your answers and working in this test paper.

- Check your work carefully before the end of the test.

- If you're not sure what to do, ask your teacher.

Instructions

 This means write down your answer or show your working and your answer.

 You may use a calculator in this test.

Formulas

Trapezium

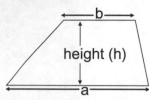

Area = $\dfrac{(a + b)}{2} \times h$

Prism

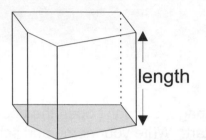

length

Volume = area of cross-section × length

---

1. Calculate the value of each of the expressions below when x = -2.

(a) $4 + x =$ ....

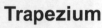

1 mark

(b) $5x =$ ....

1 mark

(c) $2x^2 =$ ....

1 mark

2. I am going on holiday and need to buy some euros.

    BetaTravel offers 82 euros for £60

    BestXchange offers 100 euros for £72

(a) Which gives the better value for money?
     You must show your working.

     ....   ☐ 2 marks

(b) Calculate how many euros I would get for £100 at BestXChange.

     .... euros   ☐ 1 mark

3. Look at the diagram. The lines marked with arrows are parallel.
PQ and QR are the same length.

(DIAGRAM NOT
TO SCALE)

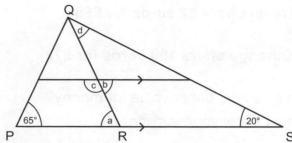
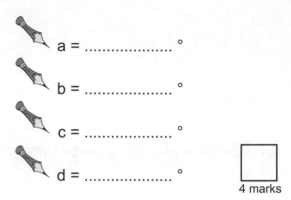

Work out the size of the angles a, b, c and d.

a = ... °

b = ... °

c = ... °

d = ... °

4 marks

4. (a) Write down the nth term for this number sequence:

1, 4, 9, 16, 25, ...

....

1 mark

Use your answer to work out the nth term for these number sequences:

(b) **2, 5, 10, 17, 26, ...**

....

1 mark

(c) **3, 12, 27, 48, 75, ...**

....

1 mark

(d) **3, 9, 19, 33, 51, ...**

....

1 mark

5. A goat has a rope attached to its collar.

The length of the rope is 6 metres.

The other end of the rope is attached to the outside of the shed as shown.

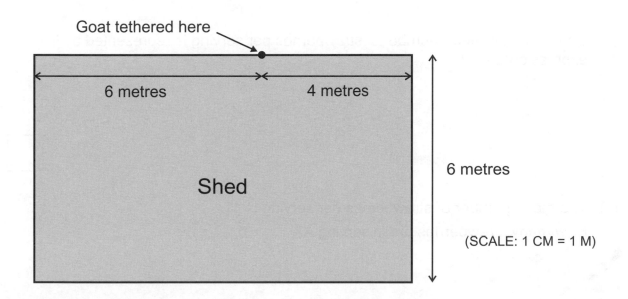

Goat tethered here

6 metres

4 metres

Shed

6 metres

(SCALE: 1 CM = 1 M)

Show accurately on the diagram the region where the goat could be.

Label the region R.

2 marks

6. Joe buys 3 servings of strawberries at the Wimbledon Lawn Tennis Championships.
The number of strawberries in each serving are given by the expressions below.

Serving	Number of strawberries
A	2n
B	n + 5
C	3n – 2

(a) Write an expression for the total number of strawberries in the
3 servings. Show your working.

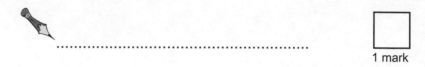

....

1 mark

(b) Show that the mean number of strawberries per serving is represented by the
expression 2n + 1.

1 mark

(c) The mean number of strawberries per serving is 11.
How many strawberries are in serving A?

....

2 marks

7. I have three coins — a 2p, a 5p and a 10p.

    The 2p and 5p coins are equally likely to show a head or a tail.

    The 10p coin is biased so it is twice as likely to show a head as a tail.

    I throw all three coins.

    What is the probability I get the same on all of them?

....

3 marks

8. Harry has started weight-training.

    Since he started, his weight has increased by $\dfrac{1}{16}$.
    He now weighs 76.5 kg.

    How much did he weigh before he started?

.... kg

2 marks

9. In the table below there are statements on the left hand side and expressions for someone's age, in years, on the right hand side.

The letter B represents Bill's age in years.

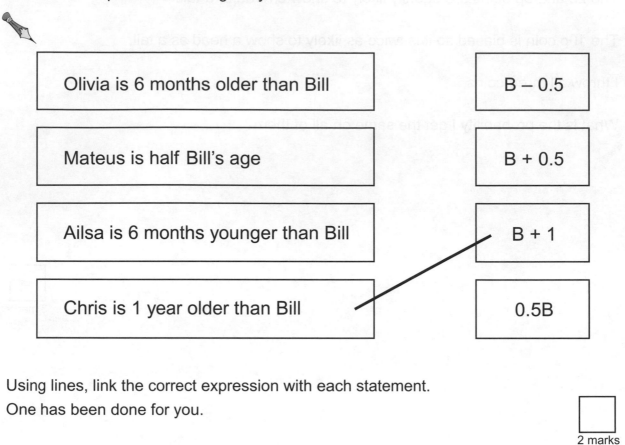

Olivia is 6 months older than Bill	B − 0.5
Mateus is half Bill's age	B + 0.5
Ailsa is 6 months younger than Bill	B + 1
Chris is 1 year older than Bill	0.5B

Using lines, link the correct expression with each statement.

One has been done for you.

2 marks

10. Multiply out the expressions below.

Write your answers as simply as possible.

(a) $3(x - 3) - 2(3 - 2x)$

....

2 marks

(b) $(2x - 1)(x - 3)$

....

2 marks

11. Anjum, Billie and Catie are eating sweets.

The ratio of the number Anjum eats to the number Billie eats is 3 : 5.
The ratio of the number Billie eats to the number Catie eats is 4 : 7.
Catie eats 70 sweets.

How many sweets do the three children eat altogether?

....

2 marks

12. Fill in the missing numbers:

(a) 150 mm is the same as .... m.

1 mark

(b) 150 mm² is the same as .... m².

1 mark

(c) The length of a piece of wood is 150 mm to the nearest 10 mm.

The actual length lies between .... mm and .... mm.

1 mark

13. The frequency table shows the number of days that 30 pupils were off sick from school in a year.

Number of days sick	Frequency
0 - 4	14
5 - 9	8
10 - 14	5
15 - 19	3

(a) Which is the modal group?

....

1 mark

(b) Estimate the mean number of days that pupils were off sick.

....

3 marks

(c) Explain why you can only find an estimate of the mean.

1 mark

14. Some exam-markers get paid £2 for each paper they mark.

Anna takes 20 minutes to mark each paper.
David takes 15 minutes to mark each paper.

(a) Work out how much Anna and David earn per hour.

 Anna earns £.................... per hour

 David earns £.................... per hour

1 mark

(b) Use your answers to part (a) to plot two points on the grid below.

By plotting at least two more points, draw a graph to show the relationship between amount earned per hour and the time taken to mark each paper.

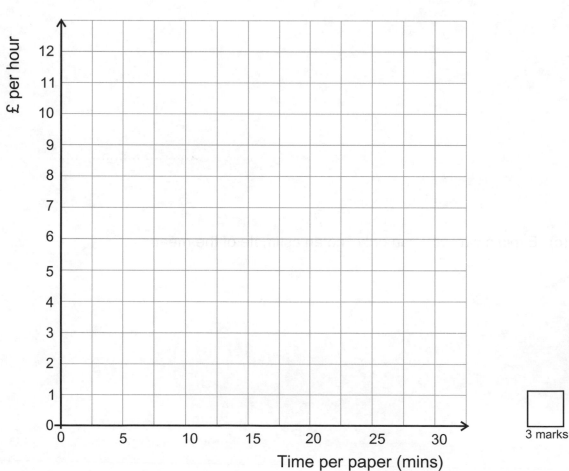

3 marks

15. (a) In a test, Jamie answered 40% of the questions.

He got 50% of the questions he answered right.

Manjinder answered 50% of the questions and got 40% of them right.

Manjinder said "That means we got the same mark."

Is Manjinder right or wrong? Explain your answer.

$\square$ 2 marks

(b) In a sale, a shop reduced all its prices by 10%.

After the sale, the shop manager increased the prices by 10%.

A customer said "That means the prices are now the same as they were before the sale."

Is the customer right or wrong? Explain your answer.

$\square$ 2 marks

(c) At Mary's local garage, the price of a litre of petrol rose by 20% in April, then by another 20% in May.

Mary said "That's a 40% rise in two months."

Is Mary right or wrong? Explain your answer.

$\square$ 2 marks

16. David reads in the paper that the dice produced at one factory are more likely to land on a six than on any of the other numbers.

To investigate this he buys 20 dice.
He throws all 20 dice together 12 times.
He counts the number of sixes he gets each time.

The table shows his results.

Throw	1	2	3	4	5	6	7	8	9	10	11	12
Number of sixes	1	3	5	2	4	6	3	4	6	0	4	4

(a) Use David's results to estimate the probability of getting a six using these dice.

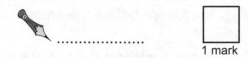

.... ⬜ 1 mark

(b) David decides from his investigation that the paper is right.

Do you agree? Explain your answer.

⬜ 1 mark

17. The diagram shows the cross-section of a marquee fixed on horizontal ground.

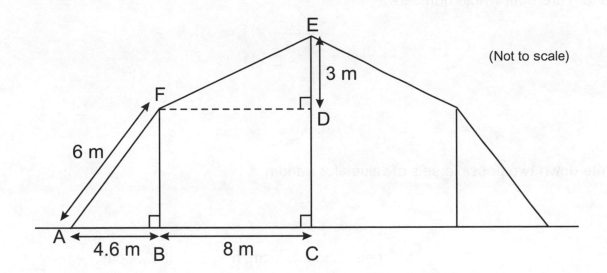

(Not to scale)

BF and CE are vertical supports.

AB = 4.6 m, AF = 6 m, DE = 3 m and BC = 8 m.

(a) Which expression represents the length of EF in metres?
Circle the correct answer.

$3^2 + 8^2$ $\sqrt{3^2 + 8^2}$ $\sqrt{(3 + 8)^2}$ $\sqrt{3} + \sqrt{8}$ $\sqrt{3^2 - 8^2}$

1 mark

(b) Work out the length of BF to 3 significant figures.

.... cm

2 marks

18. A cylinder has radius r, height h, and a volume of 36π cm³.
r and h are both whole numbers.

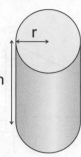

Write down two possible sets of values for r and h.

r =................... cm, h =................... cm

or r =................... cm, h =................... cm

19. In the diagram below, triangles ABE and ACD are similar.

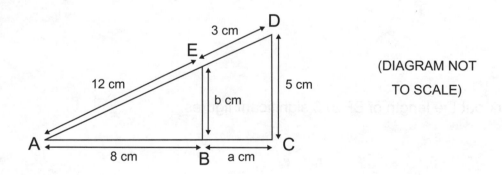

(DIAGRAM NOT TO SCALE)

Find the lengths a and b.

a = ... cm

b = ... cm

END OF TEST

Key Stage 3

Science Test

Practice Paper 1A

Read this page, but don't open the booklet until your teacher says you can start. Write your name and school in the spaces below.

First Name _____

Last Name _____

School _____

Remember

- You have one hour to do the paper.

- Make sure you have these things with you before you start:
  pen, pencil, rubber, ruler, angle measurer or protractor,
  calculator.

- The easier questions are at the start of the paper.

- Try to answer all of the questions.

- Don't use any rough paper — write all your answers
  and working in this test paper.

- Check your work carefully.

- If you're not sure what to do, ask your teacher.

1. The diagram below shows the carbon cycle.

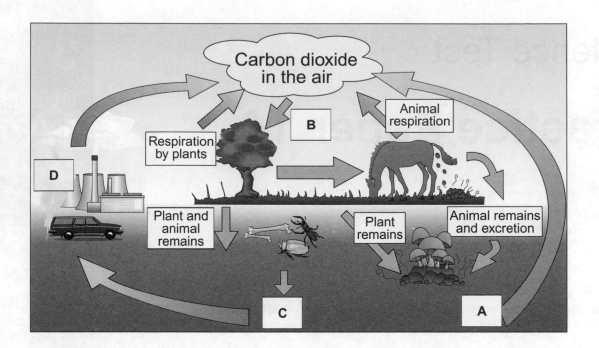

(a) Write the letters from the diagram that represent each of the following statements.

(i) Carbon compounds in fossil fuels like coal, oil and natural gas. ....

(ii) Decomposers release carbon dioxide into the air. ....

(iii) Photosynthesis by plants. ....

3 marks

(b) What does letter D on the diagram represent?

....

1 mark

Maximum 4 marks

2.   Tim is investigating how quickly a cup of tea cools down with different amounts of tea in the cup.

(a)   What factor would Tim need to change as he carried out his investigation (the independent variable)?

....

1 mark

(b)   What factor would Tim need to measure as he carried out his investigation (the dependent variable)?

....

1 mark

(c)   Write down one factor Tim would need to keep the same to make his investigation a fair test.

....

....

1 mark

Maximum 3 marks

3. The diagram shows the arrangement of particles in water as it changes state.

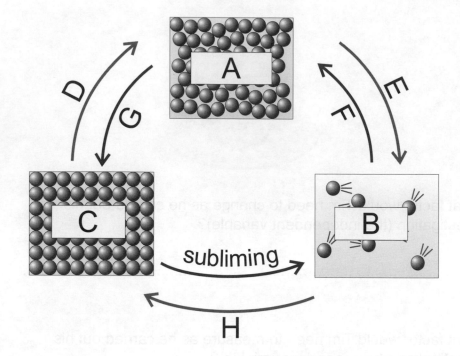

(a) Write the correct letter from the diagram next to each term below.

    (i)   Solid   ....

    (ii)   Melting   ....

    (iii)   Condensing   ....

    (iv)   Liquid   ....

    (v)   Freezing   ....

    (vi)   Gas   ....

    (vii)   Boiling   ....

7 marks

(b) Give one change of state during which energy is given out.

....

1 mark

Maximum 8 marks

4. Suzanne is looking at a cup.
Light is shining onto the cup.

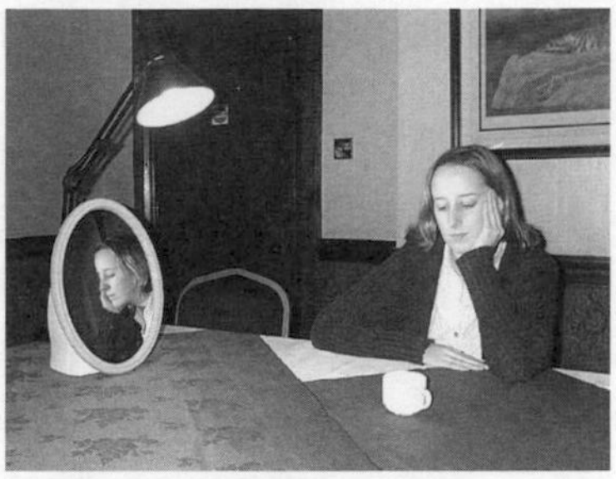

(a) Describe how light from the lamp lights
up the cup so Suzanne can see it.

....

....

....

2 marks

(b) Suzanne looks at different coloured cups in different colours of light.
Fill in the empty boxes in the table to show what colour the cups appear to her.

colour of cup	white	blue
colour of light	red	white
colour of cup to Suzanne		

2 marks

(c) Why does a black object look black in any light?

....

1 mark

(d) In the diagram, measure the following:

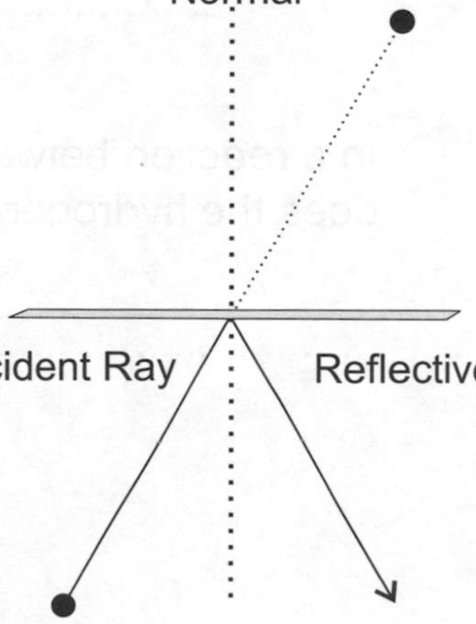

(i) The angle of incidence

....

(ii) The angle of reflection

....

(iii) The distance from the object to the mirror

....

(iv) The distance from the image to the mirror

....

Normal

Incident Ray   Reflective Ray

4 marks

Maximum 9 marks

5. Some metals react with acids to produce metal salts and hydrogen gas.

(a) Draw lines to join each of the metal salts below with the metal and the acid that could have reacted to produce it.

METAL	METAL SALT	ACID	
zinc	lead chloride	sulfuric acid	☐ 1 mark
iron	zinc nitrate	hydrochloric acid	☐ 1 mark
lead	iron sulfate	nitric acid	☐ 1 mark

(b) (i) What could you use to determine the pH of an acid?

.... ☐
1 mark

(ii) What would be observed in this pH test?

.... ☐
1 mark

(c) In a reaction between a metal and an acid, which reactant does the hydrogen gas that is produced come from?

.... ☐
1 mark

Maximum 6 marks

6. The diagram below shows a plant cell.

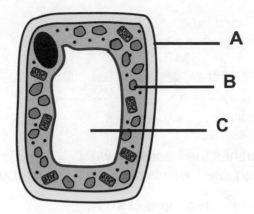

(a)   Give the correct names for the structures labelled on the diagram.

A   ....

B   ....

C   ....

3 marks

(b)   What is the function of structure A?

....

1 mark

(c)   Sarah was looking at the root cells of a plant under the microscope.
Why did the cells have no structures like structure B?

....

....

2 marks

Maximum 6 marks

7. Workers in a shoe factory use a tool to make holes in the leather.

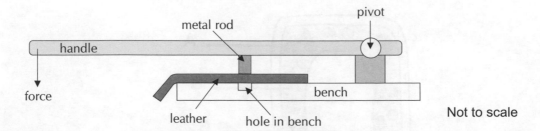

To punch a hole, a worker pushes the handle down.
If the force is not large enough, the tool will not punch the leather.

A worker pushes on the handle with a force of 40 N.
The following diagram shows the force on the handle.

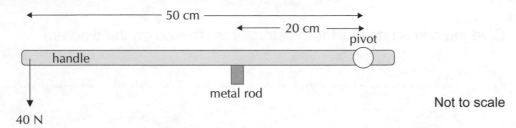

(a) Calculate the moment (turning effect) of the 40 N force applied to the end of the handle. Show your working and write down the units.

....

....

2 marks

(b) The moment pushes the metal rod onto the leather.
What force does the rod apply to the leather?

....

....

1 mark

(c) A different worker uses the punch.
The metal rod pushes on the leather with a force of 80 N.

The end of the metal rod has an area of 0.5 cm^2.
What pressure does the rod exert on the leather? Write down the units.

....

....

2 marks

Maximum 5 marks

8. Four metals were added to cold water and to dilute hydrochloric acid.
The results are shown in the table below.

metal	with dilute hydrochloric acid	with cold water
nickel	some bubbles of gas form if the acid is warm	no reaction
potassium	(cannot be done safely)	floats, then melts, a flame appears, and sometimes there's an explosion
platinum	no reaction	no reaction
zinc	bubbles of gas form and metal dissolves slowly	no reaction

(a)   Write the names of the **four** metals in order of reactivity.

.... (most reactive)

....

....

.... (least reactive)

2 marks

(b)   Name another metal, that is not in the table,
which reacts in a similar way to potassium.

....

1 mark

Continued over the page

(c)   Two test tubes have been set up as shown in the diagram below.

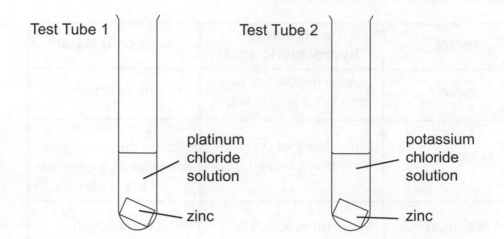

Test Tube 1 — platinum chloride solution — zinc

Test Tube 2 — potassium chloride solution — zinc

Nothing happened in Test Tube 2.
In Test Tube 1, the zinc was gradually covered with a grey deposit.

(i)   What was the grey deposit that formed in Test Tube 1?

....

1 mark

(ii)   Why did no reaction take place in Test Tube 2?

....

....

1 mark

Maximum 5 marks

9.   All cigarette packets sold in Britain are now printed with a government health warning.

Smoking kills

(a)   Tar is a chemical found in cigarette smoke.
Describe two health problems caused by tar.

1 ....

2 ....

2 marks

The table below shows the percentages of low birth weight babies who had mothers who smoked during pregnancy.

Baby's mass at birth (kg)	2.25 or less	2.26 – 2.70	2.71 – 3.15	3.16 – 3.60	3.61 – 4.05	over 4.05
% of mothers who smoked	50	42	36	29	21	20

(b)   Plot this information as a bar chart below.

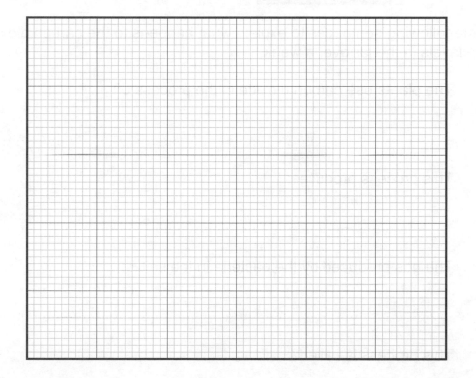

3 marks

(c)   Low birth weight has been linked with health problems in babies.
Use your bar chart to suggest why women are advised not to smoke while they are pregnant.

....

....

1 mark

Maximum 6 marks

10. John uses his empty king-size peanut butter jar to make a garden.
He keeps it in a brightly lit room with the sealed lid on.

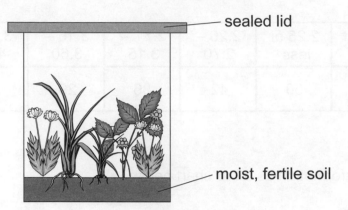

sealed lid

moist, fertile soil

Complete the following sentences to explain what happens to the carbon dioxide and oxygen levels in the jar over a week.

(a)　(i)　The plants use carbon dioxide in the process of:

....

1 mark

(ii)　This process produces:

....

1 mark

(iii)　The gas produced by the bacteria in the soil is:

....

1 mark

(iv)　This process is called:

....

1 mark

(b)   Plants cross-pollinate by transferring pollen from one plant to another.

Give two reasons why this is more likely to happen in a normal outdoor garden than in the bottled garden.

1 ....

....

2 ....

....

2 marks

Maximum 6 marks

---

11.   Stefan held a piece of magnesium ribbon with tongs and placed it in a hot Bunsen flame. He saw it burn with a bright flame and produce a white ash.

magnesium ribbon

(a)   Write down one observation that showed that a chemical reaction had taken place.

....

1 mark

(b)   What is the chemical name for the white ash produced?

....

1 mark

(c)   Write a word equation for the chemical reaction that took place.

....

1 mark

Maximum 3 marks

12. The diagram shows a fractional distillation column used in a laboratory to separate crude oil into its different parts (called fractions).

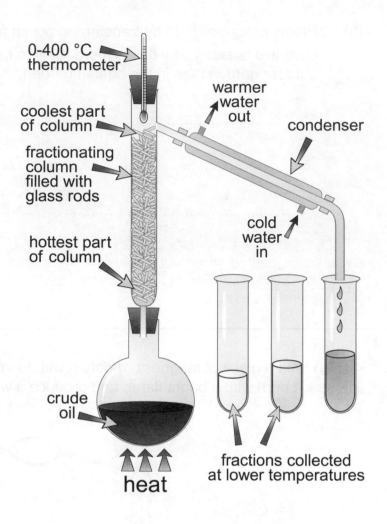

0-400 °C thermometer

coolest part of column

fractionating column filled with glass rods

hottest part of column

warmer water out

condenser

cold water in

crude oil

fractions collected at lower temperatures

heat

(a) Put a tick in the box next to the best description of crude oil below.

☐ A pure element ☐ A pure compound

☐ A mixture of elements ☐ A mixture of compounds

1 mark

(b) The fraction being collected in the diagram is a substance called naphtha.

(i) What physical state is naphtha in while it's in the fractionating column?

....

1 mark

(ii) Explain how the condenser works to cause the naphtha to change state.

....

1 mark

Maximum 3 marks

13. Shahana set up the following experiment to investigate the effect of light intensity on photosynthesis. Her results are shown in the table.

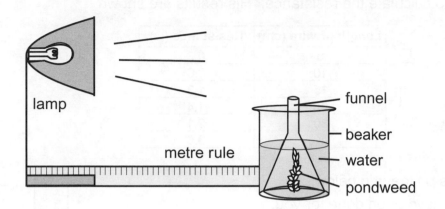

Distance of lamp from beaker (cm)	Number of bubbles produced by pondweed in 1 minute
100	2
80	5
60	9
40	20
20	39

(a) Plot the results of this experiment on the axes below.
Draw a smooth curve through the points and label the axes.

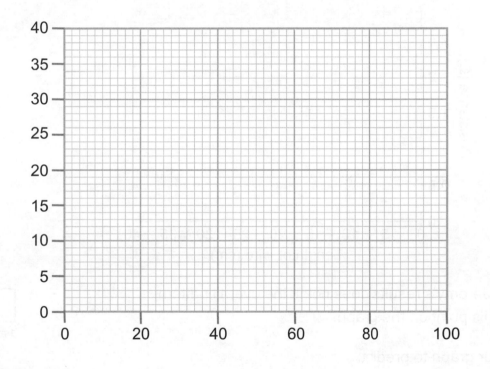

3 marks

(b) What conclusions could Shahana draw from her results?

....

....

2 marks

Maximum 5 marks

14. Jeremy used the following circuit to investigate the resistance of different lengths of wire. For each different length of wire, he measured the voltage and the current and used these to calculate the resistance. His results are shown in the table.

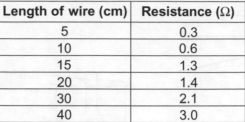

Length of wire (cm)	Resistance (Ω)
5	0.3
10	0.6
15	1.3
20	1.4
30	2.1
40	3.0

(a) (i) Plot the results on the grid below.
The first three have been done for you.

☐ 1 mark

(ii) Draw a line of best fit.

☐ 1 mark

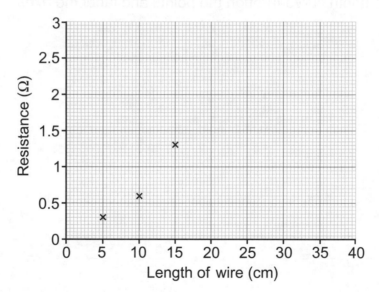

(b) One of Jeremy's results does not fit the overall pattern.
Circle this point on the graph.

☐ 1 mark

(c) Use your graph to predict:

(i) the resistance of a wire that is 25 cm long. .... Ω

☐ 1 mark

(ii) the length of a wire with the resistance 2.5 Ω. .... cm

☐ 1 mark

(d) Describe the relationship between resistance and wire length.

....

☐ 1 mark

Maximum 6 marks

END OF TEST

Key Stage 3

Science Test

Practice Paper 1B

Science

KEY STAGE 3

PRACTICE PAPER 1B

Read this page, but don't open the booklet until your teacher says you can start. Write your name and school in the spaces below.

First Name _____

Last Name _____

School _____

Remember

☐ You have one hour to do the paper.

☐ Make sure you have these things with you before you start: pen, pencil, rubber, ruler, angle measurer or protractor, calculator.

☐ The easier questions are at the start of the paper.

☐ Try to answer all of the questions.

☐ Don't use any rough paper — write all your answers and working in this test paper.

☐ Check your work carefully.

☐ If you're not sure what to do, ask your teacher.

1. Neil is making syrup by dissolving sugar in water in a beaker.

(a) Identify the solvent, solution and solute.

     (i)   Solvent   ....

     (ii)   Solution   ....

     (iii) Solute   ....

3 marks

(b) Suggest one thing Neil could do to the mixture
to get more sugar to dissolve.

....

1 mark

Maximum 4 marks

2. Draw lines to match the parts of the body with the function they carry out in human digestion.

Small intestine		absorbs the water from the food waste.
Stomach		absorbs nutrients into the bloodstream.
Teeth		churns up food and mixes it with acid and enzymes.
Large intestine		moves food to the next part of the digestive system by peristalsis.
Gullet		stores waste water.
		grind up food and mix it with saliva.

5 marks

Maximum 5 marks

3. The particles that make up various substances are shown below.

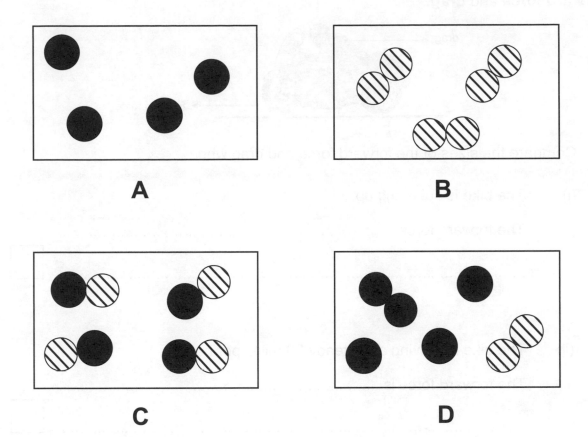

Complete the table by writing the letter of each diagram opposite its correct description.

Description	Letter
An element made up of molecules	
Molecules in a compound	
A mixture of different elements	
An element made up of atoms	

3 marks

Maximum 3 marks

4. James rides a motorbike to work every day. Two horizontal forces affect its motion: **forward force** and **drag**.

drag

forward force

(a) Compare the sizes of the forward force and drag when:

(i) The bike is speeding up.

The forward force is ....

....

1 mark

(ii) The bike is moving at a steady 30 miles per hour.

The forward force is ....

....

1 mark

(iii) The bike is slowing down.

The forward force is ....

....

1 mark

(b) The forward force occurs because the tyres are **not** able to spin on the road. What force prevents them slipping?

....

1 mark

Maximum 4 marks

5. The levels of various gases in the atmosphere vary over time, partly due to the action of green plants. During the day plants photosynthesise. Photosynthesis can be represented by the following equation:

$$\text{gas B} + \text{water} \xrightarrow[\text{CHLOROPHYLL}]{\text{LIGHT}} \text{glucose} + \text{gas A}$$

(a) Name gas A and gas B.

Gas A ....

Gas B ....

2 marks

At night photosynthesis stops but plants still carry out another chemical reaction which affects the levels of the two gases.

(b) What is the name of this reaction?

....

1 mark

(c) Write down the word equation for this reaction.

....

1 mark

Maximum 4 marks

6. Matilda is making different salts by mixing together different combinations of acids and alkalis. Name the salt produced when Matilda mixes:

(a) nitric acid and potassium hydroxide.

....

1 mark

(b) sulfuric acid and sodium hydroxide.

....

1 mark

(c) hydrochloric acid and calcium hydroxide.

....

1 mark

Maximum 3 marks

7. Keith wants to find out which snack has the highest energy content. He does an experiment to look at the amount of energy in two brands of crisps.

He burns a sample of the food to see how much this raises the temperature of the water in the test tube. This rise in temperature uses energy from the food.

(a) Suggest two things Keith should have done to make the experiment a fair test:

1. ....

2. ....

☐ 2 marks

(b) Keith should also take some precautions to increase the safety of the experiment. Give two things he could do to make the experiment safer.

1. ....

2. ....

☐ 2 marks

(c) The table shows nutritional details from the packets of the different brands.

	energy in kJ	protein in g	carbohydrate in g	fat in g	fibre in g
100 g of Runners' plain crisps	2050	6.2	56.2	28.7	4.2
100 g of Henry's Health Snack	1300	9.2	45.1	10.5	9.1

Keith repeats his experiment using 10 grams of each brand.
Write down the letter of the correct statement.

A: The temperature will rise more with the Runners' Crisps.

B: The temperature change will be the same.

C: The temperature will rise more with the Henry's Health snack.

The correct statement is statement ....

☐ 1 mark

(d) Neither snack contains vitamin C. Give an example of a type of food which provides a good source of vitamin C.

....

☐ 1 mark

(e) (i) Why is fibre an important part of a balanced diet?

....

....

(ii) Using the table, give **two** reasons why Henry's Health Snacks are healthier than Runners' plain crisps.

....

....

Maximum 9 marks

---

8. The diagram shows the rock cycle. Write the correct letter from the diagram next to each of the labels given below.

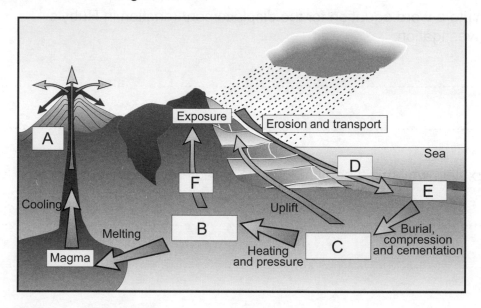

Label	**Letter**
(a) Metamorphic rocks	....
(b) Igneous rocks	....
(c) Deposition	....
(d) Sediments	....
(e) Sedimentary rocks	....

Maximum 5 marks

9. Ruby is investigating displacement reactions.
The diagram shows her experiment and its results.

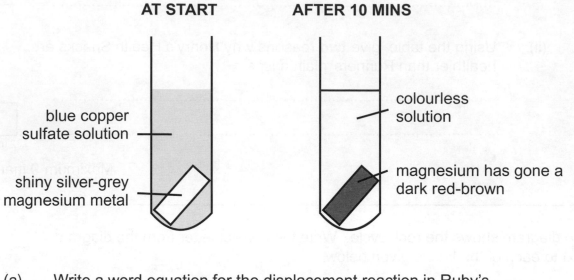

AT START   **AFTER 10 MINS**

blue copper sulfate solution

shiny silver-grey magnesium metal

colourless solution

magnesium has gone a dark red-brown

(a) Write a word equation for the displacement reaction in Ruby's investigation.

....

....

2 marks

(b) Explain why this type of reaction is called a displacement reaction.

....

....

1 mark

(c) Which of the two metals involved in the reaction was the more reactive?

....

1 mark

Maximum 4 marks

10. Peter lives in England. He is talking on the telephone to his friend Manuel, who lives in Ecuador. Ecuador is a country which lies on the Earth's equator.

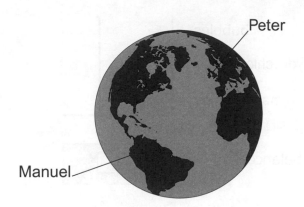

Peter says, "It's summer here. The days are eighteen hours long and it gets really hot — 25 °C sometimes."

Manuel says, "The days are always about twelve hours long here and the temperature often reaches 35 °C."

(a)   When it's summer in England, why does England have longer days than Ecuador?

....

....

2 marks

(b)   Having longer days is one reason why it gets hot in summer in England. Explain another reason why it gets hot in summer in England.

....

....

2 marks

Maximum 4 marks

11. Jill did an experiment to investigate how quickly marble chips dissolve in different concentrations of hydrochloric acid. As the reaction proceeded she recorded the mass of the beaker containing the reaction mixture at five minute intervals. The apparatus she used is shown below.

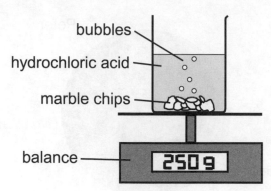

bubbles

hydrochloric acid

marble chips

balance — 250 g

(a) What factor did Jill change as she carried out her investigation (the independent variable)?

....

1 mark

(b) Give two factors she should have kept the same to make it a fair test.

1. ....

2. ....

2 marks

(c) What could Jill do to make her results more reliable?

....

....

1 mark

(d) The table shows the results obtained from Jill's first experiment. She used 220 g of marble chips.

Time (mins)	Mass of beaker and contents (g)
0	250.0
5	245.0
10	242.0
15	240.5
20	239.5
25	239.5

(i)   Draw a fully labelled graph to show these results on the grid below,
       joining the points with a smooth curve.

3 marks

(ii)   Describe the trend shown by the results.

       ....

1 mark

(iii) The reaction stopped at one of the times listed below.
       Tick the correct box.

       ☐ 14 minutes   ☐ 18½ minutes

       ☐ 22½ minutes   ☐ 25 minutes

1 mark

(iv)   By how much did the mass of the beaker and its contents
       decrease in 25 minutes?

       ....

2 marks

Maximum 11 marks

12. At a theatre red, green and blue spotlights are used.

An actress is wearing a yellow dress. However, when the red and blue spotlights shine on her, the dress appears red.

(a) Explain why the dress appears red when only the red and blue spotlights are shining on it.

....

....

2 marks

(b) When only a red and a green spotlight are shining on it, the dress appears yellow. Explain why.

....

....

2 marks

(c) Predict what colour the dress would look when all three lights are used.

....

1 mark

Maximum 5 marks

13. When Liam fell off his bike, he dislocated his shoulder. A doctor examined Liam's shoulder joint and the muscle surrounding it.

(a) Muscles work in antagonistic pairs. What does this mean?

....

....

2 marks

The diagram shows the bones and muscles in the arm.

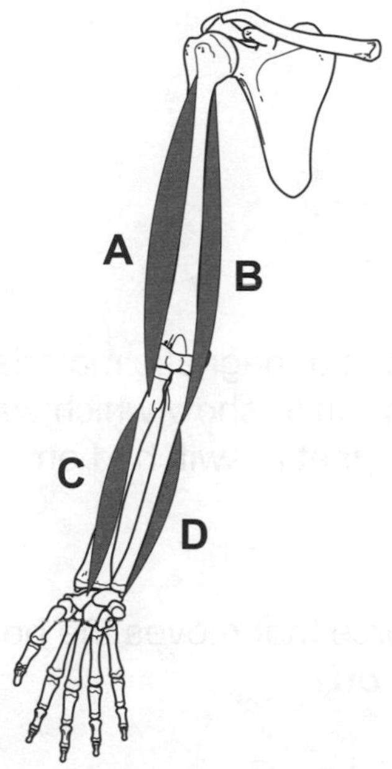

(b) Which of the muscles in the diagram, **A**, **B**, **C** or **D**, contracts to bend the arm at the elbow?

....

1 mark

Maximum 3 marks

14. The diagram shows an electromagnet used to control a device for locking a door.

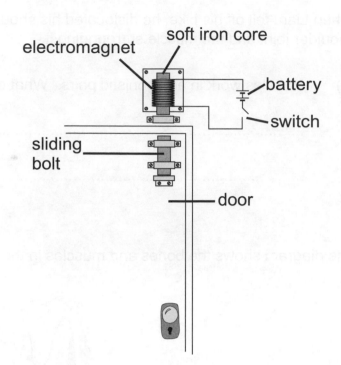

When the electromagnet is switched on, the door is locked.

When the electromagnet is switched off, the door is unlocked.

(a) The sliding bolt is made from a magnetic material.
Draw an arrow on the diagram to show which way the sliding bolt moves when the electromagnet is switched on.

1 mark

(b) What is the name of the force that moves the bolt when the electromagnet is switched **off**?

....

1 mark

(c) Suggest a material the bolt could be made from.

....

1 mark

(d) Write down one way of making the electromagnet stronger.

....

1 mark

Maximum 4 marks

15. Read the following description of a garden ecosystem and answer the questions that follow.

> The 'cabbage white' butterfly feeds on brassica plants. It shares this food source with slugs and snails, but the slugs and snails will also eat lettuce. Small birds like blue tits and thrushes eat the butterflies, slugs and snails. Cats eat the blue tits and the thrushes.

(a)   Draw out the food web in the space provided.

3 marks

(b)   Why is it harder to collect reliable data when working in the field than when working in the laboratory? Tick the correct box.

☐   It's hard to get a large enough sample.

☐   There are many variables that cannot be controlled when working in the field.

☐   Scientists cannot record their data properly when they work outdoors.

1 mark

Continued over the page

(c)   Suggest a way that slugs and snails could be counted in a garden.

....

1 mark

(d)   A gardener uses slug pellets to kill slugs and snails, to stop them eating his plants.

Describe and explain the effect you would expect this to have on the number of blue tits in the garden.

....

....

....

2 marks

Maximum 7 marks

END OF TEST

Key Stage 3

Science Test

Practice Paper 2A

Science

KEY STAGE
3

PRACTICE PAPER
2A

Read this page, but don't open the booklet until your teacher says you can start. Write your name and school in the spaces below.

First Name _____

Last Name _____

School _____

Remember

- You have one hour to do the paper.

- Make sure you have these things with you before you start: pen, pencil, rubber, ruler, angle measurer or protractor, calculator.

- The easier questions are at the start of the paper.

- Try to answer all of the questions.

- Don't use any rough paper — write all your answers and working in this test paper.

- Check your work carefully.

- If you're not sure what to do, ask your teacher.

1. Tick the boxes to show whether each part of the body listed below is a cell, a tissue or an organ. The first one has been done for you.

	cell	tissue	organ
Stomach	☐	☐	☑
Muscle	☐	☐	☐
Heart	☐	☐	☐
Sperm	☐	☐	☐
Brain	☐	☐	☐
Neurone	☐	☐	☐

3 marks

Maximum 3 marks

2. Digestion is the process by which food is broken down and absorbed into the bloodstream. The diagram below shows part of the digestive system.

(a) Give the name of each part labelled A to D.

A is the ....

B is the ....

C is the ....

D is the ....

4 marks

(b) Why does food need to be broken down before it is absorbed into the bloodstream?

....

1 mark

Maximum 5 marks

3. Sally has three rocks. She wants to find out what type of rock each one is.
The three types of rock are igneous, sedimentary and metamorphic.
Use the clues below to help Sally identify her rocks.

(a) Rock 1 is made of distinct layers. There is a fossil in it.

This rock is .... rock.

1 mark

(b) Rock 2 also has layers, but they are 'wavy'.
There are some small crystals visible.

This rock is .... rock.

1 mark

(c) Rock 3 has no layers and is made of lots of crystals.

This rock is .... rock.

1 mark

Maximum 3 marks

4. Animals get characteristics from their parents.

Complete the following sentences:

(a) Information about an animal's characteristics is passed on in a

molecule called ....

1 mark

(b) The female's genes are passed on in the egg.

The male's genes are passed on in the ....

1 mark

(c) The genes are held in the .... of the cells.

1 mark

(d) The process of passing characteristics by genes has a special name.

We say the children .... characteristics

from their parents.

1 mark

Maximum 4 marks

5. The diagram below shows the apparatus used to obtain pure water from impure water.

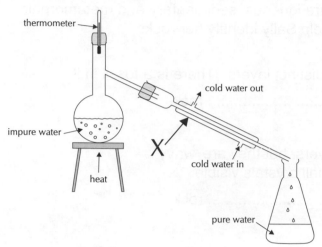

(a) What is the name of this
     process of purifying water? ....

     1 mark

(b) If you were to carry out this process, what
     temperature would the thermometer show? .... °C

     1 mark

(c) The diagram shows a piece of apparatus labelled **X**. What is its function?

     ....

     ....

     1 mark

The following diagram shows
particles in three states: solid, liquid
and gas. The arrows (1, 2, 3 and 4)
represent changes of state.

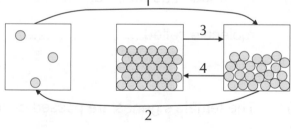

(d) Write down the names of the four changes of
     state. Choose from the words in the box.

         1 ....

         2 ....

         3 ....

         4 ....

     | condensing | melting |
     | bubbling | boiling |
     | filtering | |
     | evaporating | freezing |

     4 marks

(e) Give the number (1, 2, 3 or 4) for the change of state which occurs in
     the following places in the apparatus from parts (a), (b) and (c).

         in piece of apparatus labelled X ....

         in the flask containing impure water ....

     1 mark

                        Maximum 8 marks

6. Tina used the apparatus shown below to investigate how an electric heater heats up an aluminium block.

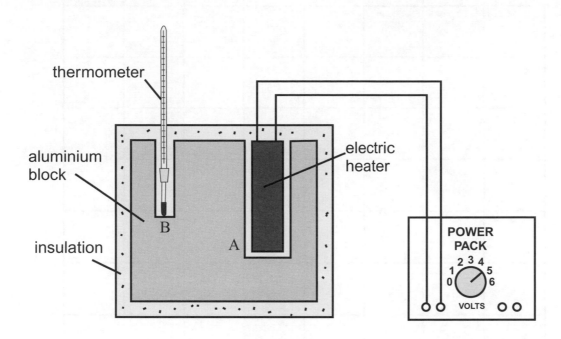

Here are her results:

Time (min)	Temperature (°C)
0	20
5	28
10	35
15	45
20	52
25	61
30	68

(a) What process causes energy from point A to reach point B?

....

1 mark

(b) Use these results to draw a graph on the grid over the page.

Decide the scale for each axis and label them clearly.
Plot the points.
Draw a line of best fit.

Continued over the page

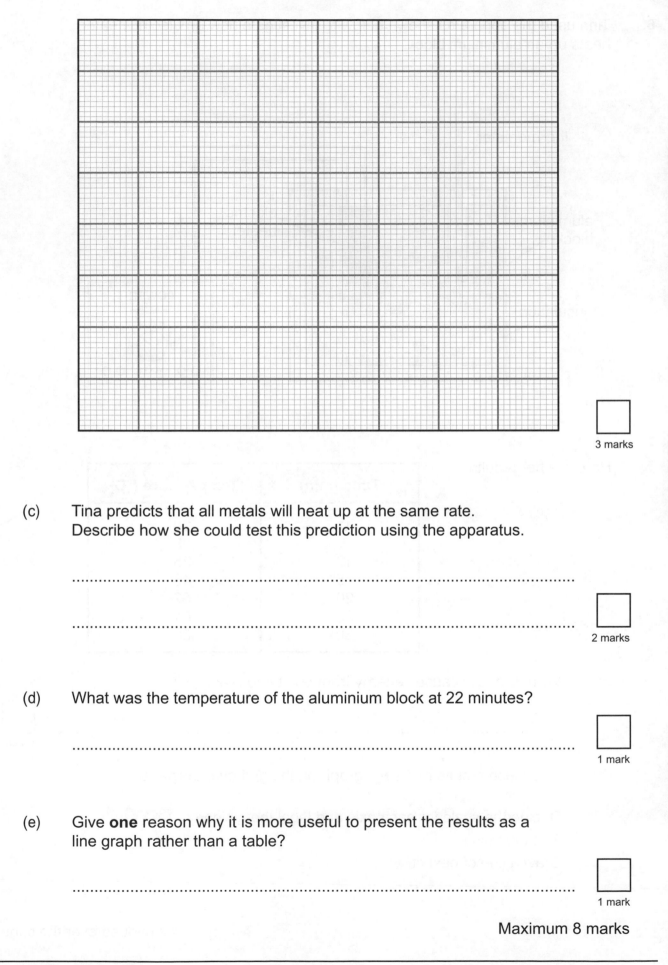

3 marks

(c) Tina predicts that all metals will heat up at the same rate.
Describe how she could test this prediction using the apparatus.

....

....

2 marks

(d) What was the temperature of the aluminium block at 22 minutes?

....

1 mark

(e) Give **one** reason why it is more useful to present the results as a
line graph rather than a table?

....

1 mark

Maximum 8 marks

7. An ice cube was placed in a beaker of water and the temperature of the water was measured every minute for 30 minutes. The water was originally at room temperature.

The results are shown on the graph below.

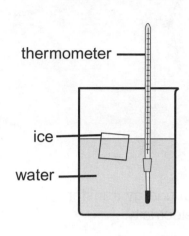 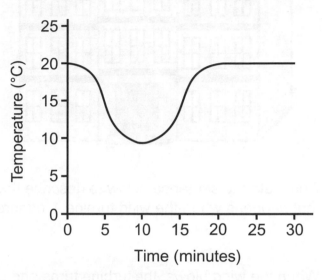

(a) What physical change do you think happened to the ice between 0 and 10 minutes?

....

(b) How did the energy of the ice particles change during this time?

....

(c) How did the energy of the water particles change during this time?

....

(d) What was the minimum temperature reached by the water?

....

(e) What was the room temperature during this experiment?

....

Maximum 5 marks

8. Newlands School has a wind turbine for generating electricity.

(a) Complete the sentence below to describe the useful energy transfer that happens when the wind turbine is generating electricity.

When the wind blows, the turbine turns and energy is stored in the

.... energy store of the turbine.

1 mark

(b) Write down one advantage of using a wind turbine to make electricity instead of using mains electricity.

....

1 mark

(c) Write down one disadvantage of using a wind turbine to make electricity instead of using mains electricity.

....

1 mark

(d) Electricity can also be created using coal, oil and gas.
What is the ultimate source of the energy that these resources contain?

....

1 mark

Maximum 4 marks

9. Jill carried out chromatography on samples of three known substances, A, B and C, and two unknown substances, X and Y.

Her results are shown in the diagram.

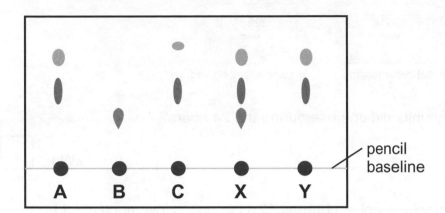

pencil baseline

A   B   C   X   Y

(a)   Which two substances are the same?

....

1 mark

(b)   Which two known substances make up substance X?

....

1 mark

(c)   Explain why the baseline is drawn in pencil and not in ink.

....

....

1 mark

(d)   Jill put the baseline above the solvent surface, not below it.
      Explain why.

....

....

1 mark

Maximum 4 marks

10. Electricity meters measure the amount of energy transferred, in units of kilowatt-hours (kWh). The diagram below shows how the meter reading in Joe's house changed over 24 hours.

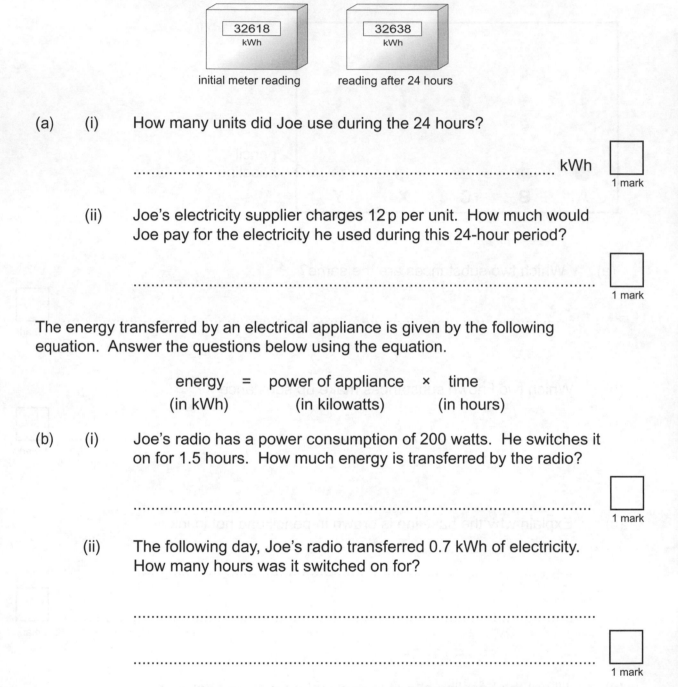

| 32618 |
| kWh |

initial meter reading

| 32638 |
| kWh |

reading after 24 hours

(a)　(i)　How many units did Joe use during the 24 hours?

.... kWh

　 1 mark

　　(ii)　Joe's electricity supplier charges 12p per unit. How much would Joe pay for the electricity he used during this 24-hour period?

....

　 1 mark

The energy transferred by an electrical appliance is given by the following equation. Answer the questions below using the equation.

energy　=　power of appliance　×　time
(in kWh)　　　　(in kilowatts)　　　(in hours)

(b)　(i)　Joe's radio has a power consumption of 200 watts. He switches it on for 1.5 hours. How much energy is transferred by the radio?

....

　 1 mark

　　(ii)　The following day, Joe's radio transferred 0.7 kWh of electricity. How many hours was it switched on for?

....

....

　 1 mark

Maximum 4 marks

11. Mr Jones has a light inside his caravan. It uses a battery.

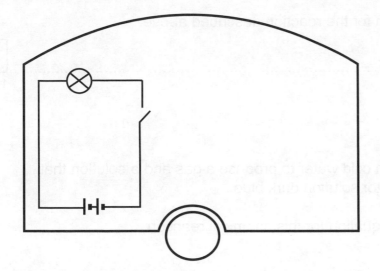

Mr Jones decides he wants another light that he can switch on when he needs it.

(a) Complete the diagram below to show how he should connect up the lights in his caravan. Include the light switches.

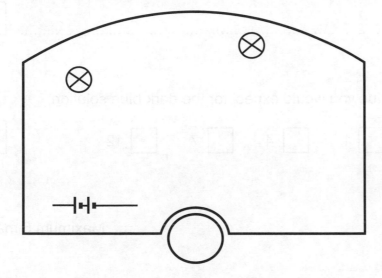

3 marks

(b) What problem might Mr Jones expect if he uses both lights in his caravan? Give a reason.

....

....

2 marks

Maximum 5 marks

12. Hot magnesium ribbon reacts with steam to produce magnesium oxide and hydrogen.

(a) Write a word equation for the reaction described above.

....

1 mark

(b) Potassium reacts with cold water to produce a gas and a solution that turns universal indicator solution dark blue.

(i) Write a word equation for this chemical reaction.

....

....

2 marks

(ii) Is the resulting solution an acid, an alkali or neutral?

....

1 mark

(iii) Tick the pH value you would expect for the dark blue solution.

☐ 0   ☐ 1   ☐ 4   ☐ 7   ☐ 12

1 mark

Maximum 5 marks

13. Plants need to take in water from the soil.
Dr Gabion decided to do an experiment to find out if there
is anything else in the soil which plants use for growth.

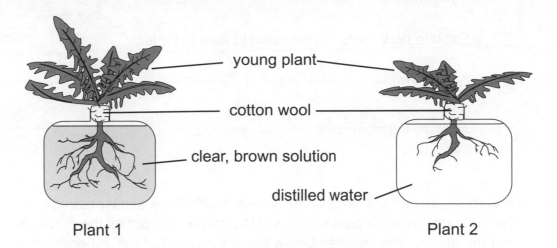

Plant 1   Plant 2

Dr Gabion made the clear, brown solution for Plant 1
by mixing up soil and water, and then separating the
soil particles out to leave the clear, brown solution.

(a)   What method could Dr Gabion use to separate the soil particles from
        the brown solution?

        ....

        ....

        1 mark

(b)   Why did Dr Gabion grow one plant in distilled water?

        ....

        ....

        1 mark

Continued over the page

(c) (i) What type of substances are in the clear, brown solution that the plant uses for growth?

....

(ii) Explain how roots are adapted to take in water.

....

....

(d) Dr Gabion carried out another experiment with three similar plants. The solutions in each container were the same. He put all the plants in a sunny place. The pictures below show the result of the experiment.

Plant 3

The container holds the clear, brown solution.
The container and leaves are wrapped in black plastic.

Plant 4

The container holds the clear, brown solution.
The leaves are wrapped in black plastic.

Plant 5

The container holds the clear, brown solution.
The container is wrapped in black plastic.

Of the three plants, Plant 5 was the only one which grew well. Explain why.

....

....

Maximum 5 marks

14. Julie is a skydiver. As she falls to Earth the forces on her change and affect her speed. Here are some possible reasons for her different speeds.

A   Her weight is greater than the air resistance.

B   Her weight is less than the air resistance.

C   Her weight is equal to the air resistance.

D   She has no weight.

E   There is no air resistance.

Choose from these reasons to explain each of the following things that happen to Julie. Write the correct letter next to each description.

What happens to Julie	Reason	
(a) When she first jumps out of the aeroplane she falls faster and faster.	....	1 mark
(b) Eventually she reaches a steady speed, moving very fast.	....	1 mark
(c) She slows down suddenly when her parachute opens.	....	1 mark
(d) She falls at a steady speed, more slowly than before.	....	1 mark

(e) Julie falls 100 metres in 15 seconds. Calculate her speed.

....

....

2 marks

Maximum 6 marks

15. Dylan compared two indigestion tablets, A and B, to see which was better at neutralising stomach acid (hydrochloric acid). The active ingredient in both tablets was calcium carbonate.

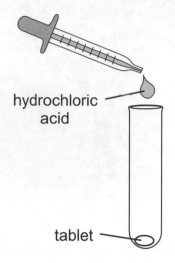

hydrochloric
acid

tablet

He put each tablet in a separate test tube and added hydrochloric acid, one drop at a time, until no further reaction occurred. He recorded the number of drops needed to neutralise each tablet.
His results are shown below.

Tablet	No. of drops needed
A	22
B	30

(a)   Which tablet was better at neutralising stomach acid?
Explain your answer.

....

2 marks

(b)   Give two factors that Dylan should have kept the same to make the comparison a fair test.

1. ....

2. ....

2 marks

(c)   What factor did Dylan change as he carried out his investigation (the independent variable)?

....

1 marks

(d)   Give one way in which Dylan could improve the experiment to make the results more reliable.

....

....

1 mark

Maximum 6 marks

END OF TEST

Key Stage 3

Science Test

Practice Paper 2B

Read this page, but don't open the booklet until your teacher says you can start. Write your name and school in the spaces below.

First Name _____

Last Name _____

School _____

Remember

☐ You have one hour to do the paper.

☐ Make sure you have these things with you before you start: pen, pencil, rubber, ruler, angle measurer or protractor, calculator.

☐ The easier questions are at the start of the paper.

☐ Try to answer all of the questions.

☐ Don't use any rough paper — write all your answers and working in this test paper.

☐ Check your work carefully.

☐ If you're not sure what to do, ask your teacher.

1. The chemical formula for a common salt is: **CuSO$_4$**

(a) Write down the names of all the elements in this compound and state how many atoms of each are present.

....

....

....

3 marks

(b) Name the salt.

....

1 mark

Maximum 4 marks

2. A double-decker bus has some mirrors to let the driver see the passengers on the top deck.

(a) On the diagram, draw the path of a ray of light to show how the driver sees the naughty child upstairs. Use a ruler.

2 marks

(b) Cyclists often use special reflectors that shine in the dark so that drivers behind them can see them. The reflector always sends light back to where it came from.

Complete the diagram to show how the reflector sends light back to where it came from.

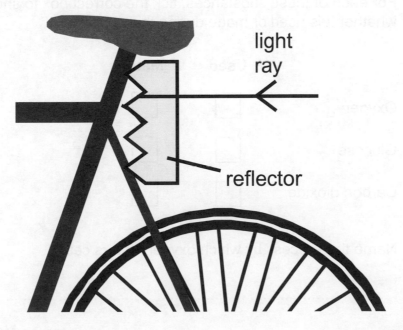

light ray

reflector

2 marks

Maximum 4 marks

3. The diagram shows a generalised human body cell.

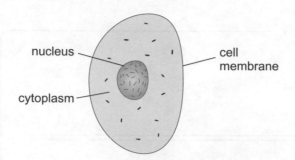

(a) Draw lines to match up the parts of the cell with their function.

| Nucleus |

| Cytoplasm |

| Cell membrane |

| controls what passes into and out of the cell. |

| controls the cell. |

| where all the chemical reactions take place. |

2 marks

(b) (i) Name the chemical process that happens in all body cells to release energy.

....

1 mark

(ii) For each of these substances, tick the correct box to show whether it is used or made during this process.

	Used	**Made**
Oxygen	☐	☐
Glucose	☐	☐
Carbon dioxide	☐	☐

3 marks

(iii) Name the process by which oxygen enters cells.

....

1 mark

Maximum 7 marks

4. The following table contains some data about different species of bird within a community.

Species of bird	Average no. of eggs laid per year by a female bird	% death rate per year
A	8	35
B	1	10
C	3	8
D	5	40
E	11	48
F	6	18

(a) Plot this information as a scatter graph on the axes below. Draw a line of best fit.

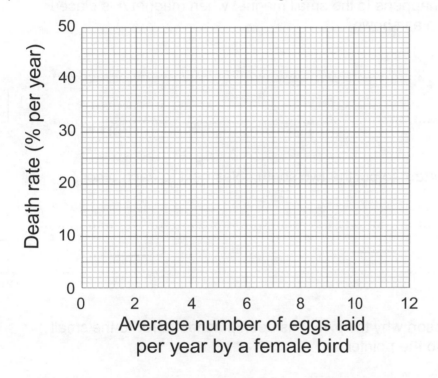

Death rate (% per year)

Average number of eggs laid per year by a female bird

3 marks

(b) Look at the graph you have plotted. Which species do you think has an unusually high death rate considering its annual egg production?

....

1 mark

(c) If 30% of bluetits die each year, use your graph to estimate the number of eggs laid per year by the average female bluetit.

....

1 mark

Maximum 5 marks

5. A pupil is using the apparatus shown below to investigate how strong different magnets are.

He tests two magnets, A and B.

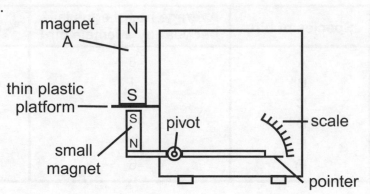

(a) Explain what happens to the small magnet when magnet A is placed on the platform as shown.

....

....

2 marks

(b) Why is it important to put the two south poles next to each other?

....

....

2 marks

(c) Suggest a reason why the pivot has been placed nearer to the small magnet than to the pointer.

....

....

1 mark

(d) How can the pupil tell which is the stronger magnet, A or B?

....

....

1 mark

Maximum 6 marks

6. Becky says that if she blows through a straw into water, the carbon dioxide in her breath will turn the water acidic. She does an experiment to test this. Her apparatus and results are shown below.

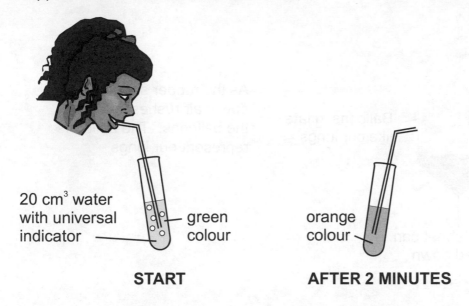

20 cm³ water with universal indicator — green colour

orange colour

START

AFTER 2 MINUTES

(a) What conclusion can you draw from Becky's results?

....

....

2 marks

(b) Huang says that Becky should have repeated the experiment using ordinary air as a control. He does this, using an air pump instead of blowing out, and finds that after two minutes the solution is still green.

What conclusion can you draw from Huang's results?

....

....

2 marks

(c) How do the two experiments support Becky's statement?

....

....

....

2 marks

Maximum 6 marks

7. A bell jar can be used to demonstrate the mechanism of breathing.

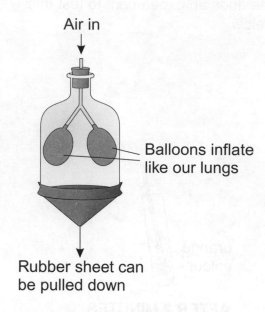

Air in

Balloons inflate like our lungs

Rubber sheet can be pulled down

As the rubber sheet is pulled down, air rushes in to fill the balloons. The balloons represent our lungs.

(a) Which part of our respiratory system does the rubber sheet represent?

....

1 mark

(b) Why does air rush in when the rubber sheet is pulled down?

....

1 mark

(c) What would happen to the balloons if the rubber sheet was then let go? Explain your answer.

....

....

2 marks

(d) Smoking can cause damage to the lungs, leading to difficulty in breathing. Name one chemical contained in cigarette smoke that can harm the lungs.

....

1 mark

Maximum 5 marks

8. The diagram shows how extrusive and intrusive igneous rocks are formed.

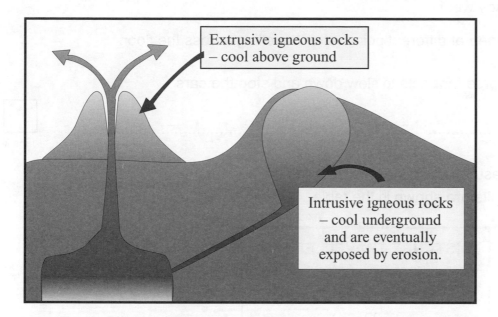

Below are diagrams showing the crystals in two igneous rock samples, A and B.

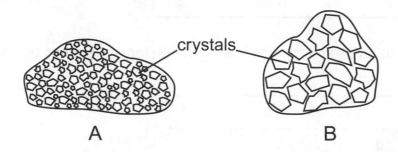

(a) Which rock sample is an intrusive igneous rock? Explain your answer.

....

....

2 marks

(b) Draw lines to connect each of the rocks below to the correct rock type.

Marble		Sedimentary
Limestone		Igneous
Granite		Metamorphic

2 marks

Maximum 4 marks

9. Mark and Bill were letting toy cars roll down a ramp onto a wooden floor to see how far they went.

The cars all stopped at different points after travelling across the floor.

(a) Name a force that acts to slow down and stop the cars.

....

(b) They measured the distances travelled by four cars.
Their results are shown in the table.

CAR	DISTANCE TRAVELLED (cm)
1	50
2	22
3	30
4	37

Complete the following bar chart showing the distance travelled by each car.

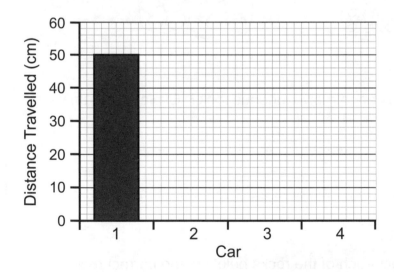

(c) Suggest three reasons why the cars travelled different distances.

....

....

Maximum 6 marks

10. Mrs Goldsmith needs to buy a light bulb. She has to choose between an ordinary 100 watt filament bulb and a 20 watt low-energy bulb. Both bulbs give out the same amount of useful energy, but the input energy is smaller for the low-energy bulb.

An advertising panel beside the low-energy bulbs says:

> A low-energy bulb only uses 20% of the energy used by an equivalent filament bulb. A low-energy bulb lasts eight times as long as a filament bulb. A low-energy bulb saves you money in the long term.

(a) What happens to the energy that is not transferred from the filament bulb by light?

....

1 mark

(b) Write down one other piece of information Mrs Goldsmith needs before she can decide whether the low-energy bulb really is cheaper in the long term.

....

....

1 mark

(c) Write down two reasons why Mrs Goldsmith might decide to buy the low-energy bulb even if it works out to be more expensive in the long run.

1. ....

2. ....

2 marks

(d) Mrs Goldsmith also needs to replace an ordinary 60 watt filament bulb. Which low-energy bulb should she choose? Tick the correct box.

☐ 20 watt   ☐ 16 watt   ☐ 12 watt   ☐ 8 watt   ☐

1 mark

Maximum 5 marks

11. This picture shows an archer.
He holds the arrow and pulls it back to fire it.

string bow
arrow

(a) At the moment shown in the picture, two **horizontal** forces act on the arrow:
the force exerted by the string and the force exerted by the archer's fingers.
The arrow **isn't** moving.

The archer pulls the arrow back and holds it with a force of 120 N.
Predict the force exerted by the string on the arrow.

...........................N

1 mark

(b) The archer releases the arrow and it moves forward. Explain why this happens.

....

....

1 mark

(c) While the arrow is flying across the field, **two** forces act on it. Gravity acts
downwards and air resistance acts in the opposite direction to the movement.
Explain why these forces **can't** balance each other, even if they are equal.

....

....

1 mark

(d) The arrow hits a target. The end of the arrow is pointed and sharp so
that it exerts a large pressure on the target.
Explain why a blunt end would exert a lower pressure on the target.

....

....

1 mark

Maximum 4 marks

12. Rahel heated 28.5 g of zinc powder in air. The mass of the white powder left behind after heating was 30.5 g.

(a) Explain why the mass of the products is never less than the mass of the reactants.

....

1 mark

(b) (i) What substance reacted with the zinc metal?

....

1 mark

(ii) Calculate the mass of this substance that reacted.

....

1 mark

(c) Write down the chemical name of the powder formed after burning.

....

1 mark

Maximum 4 marks

13. The diagram below shows "Hero's Engine". This was the first machine to demonstrate steam power. Water is boiled in the large bowl. Steam travels through the tubes supporting the revolving ball and is ejected through the two 'jets' attached to the sphere, causing it to spin.

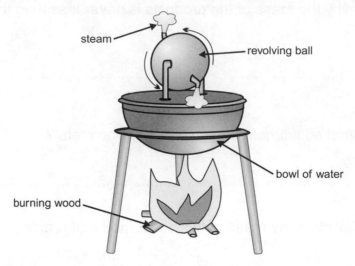

steam — revolving ball — bowl of water — burning wood

(a) What 'change of state' happens to water when it boils?

....

☐ 1 mark

(b) Starting with the energy in the wood's energy stores, describe the energy transfers that occur in Hero's Engine.

....

....

....

☐ 3 marks

(c) Wood is a renewable energy resource.
Name two non-renewable energy resources.

1. ....

2. ....

☐ 2 marks

Maximum 6 marks

14. Look at the diagram below showing part of the human skeleton.

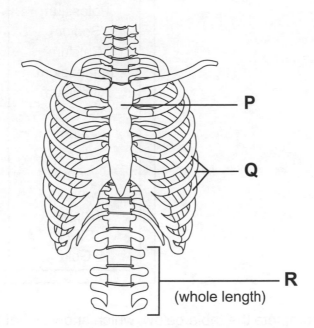

(a)   Write down the names of the structures P, Q and R in the spaces below.

P   ....

Q   ....

R   ....

(b)   The skeleton is designed for movement, support and protection.
       Which of these is the primary function of:

(i)   Structure Q? ....

(ii)   Structure R? ....

Maximum 5 marks

15. Part of the reactivity series of elements is shown on the right.

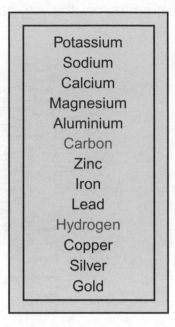

Potassium
Sodium
Calcium
Magnesium
Aluminium
Carbon
Zinc
Iron
Lead
Hydrogen
Copper
Silver
Gold

Use this information to complete the table below, which shows what happened when samples of different metals were added to solutions of various metal salts.

Use a tick (✓) to show a reaction, and a cross (✗) to show no reaction.

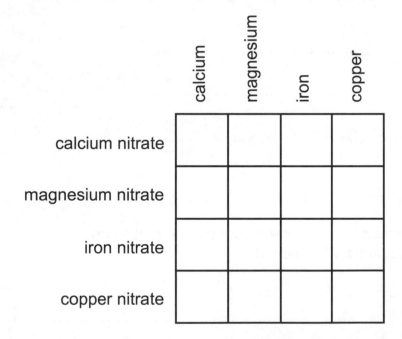

	calcium	magnesium	iron	copper
calcium nitrate				
magnesium nitrate				
iron nitrate				
copper nitrate				

4 marks

Maximum 4 marks

END OF TEST

Key Stage 3

Science Test

Practice Paper 3A

Science

KEY STAGE
3

PRACTICE PAPER
3A

Read this page, but don't open the booklet until your teacher says you can start. Write your name and school in the spaces below.

First Name _____

Last Name _____

School _____

Remember

☐ You have one hour to do the paper.

☐ Make sure you have these things with you before you start: pen, pencil, rubber, ruler, angle measurer or protractor, calculator.

☐ The easier questions are at the start of the paper.

☐ Try to answer all of the questions.

☐ Don't use any rough paper — write all your answers and working in this test paper.

☐ Check your work carefully.

☐ If you're not sure what to do, ask your teacher.

1. The diagram shows a circuit containing various different components.
Write the names of the components in the boxes next to their symbols.

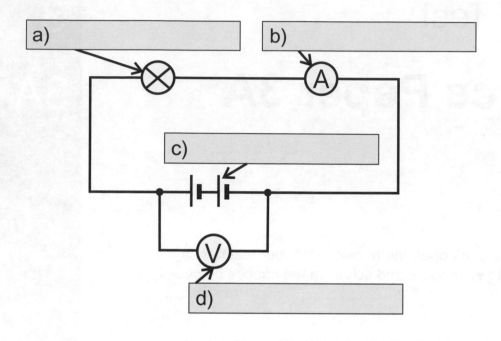

a)

b)

c)

d)

4 marks

Maximum 4 marks

---

2. Draw lines to connect each of the everyday chemicals listed below to the colour
it would turn universal indicator, and to its most likely pH value.

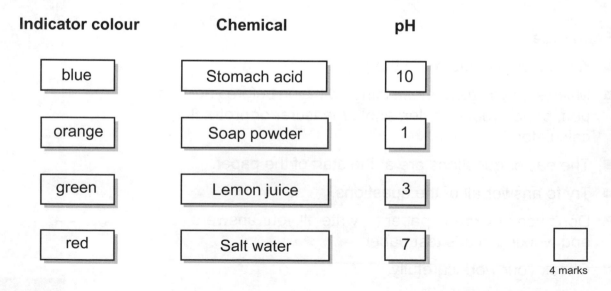

Indicator colour	Chemical	pH
blue	Stomach acid	10
orange	Soap powder	1
green	Lemon juice	3
red	Salt water	7

4 marks

Maximum 4 marks

3. (a) Choose from the words in the box below to name each part of the male reproductive system labelled on the diagram.

| sperm tube | urethra | bladder | testis | penis |

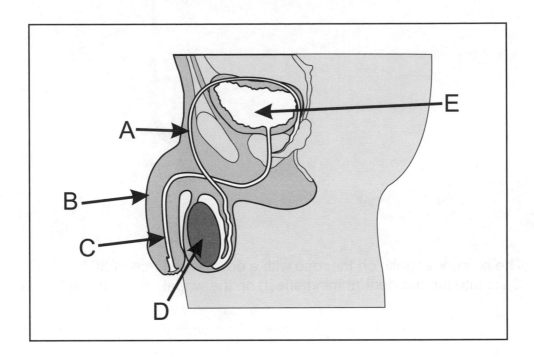

A ....

B ....

C ....

D ....

E ....

4 marks

(b) Name the sex cell produced by the male reproductive system.

....

1 mark

Maximum 5 marks

4. The picture shows a person ringing a church bell.

The bell is attached upside down to a wheel of radius 1.2 m.
To ring the bell, the rope is pulled.

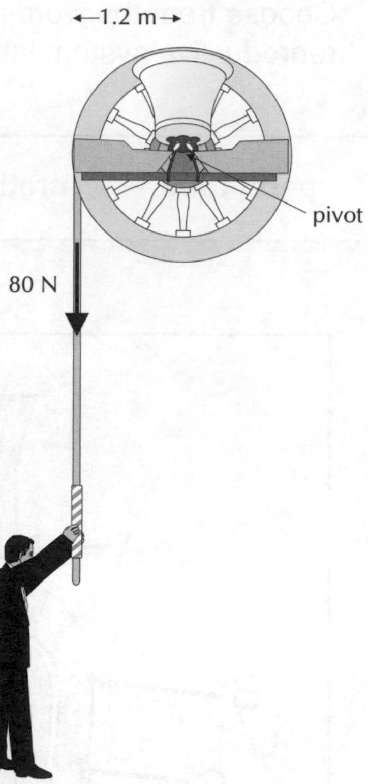

1.2 m

pivot

80 N

(a) The bell-ringer pulls on the rope with a downward force of 80 N.
Calculate the moment (turning effect) on the wheel. Write down the unit.

....

....

....

☐ 2 marks

(b) The wheel turns as the rope is pulled. When it is travelling at its highest speed, the rope moves 0.6 m in 0.05 s. Find the speed. Write down the unit.

....

....

....

☐ 2 marks

(c)   Most people can hear the sound of a bell.
       Circle the most likely frequency of a bell ringing.

300 Hz   **30 000 Hz**

3 Hz   **3 000 000 Hz**

1 mark

(d)   Energy is given out when the bell rings. This energy was originally stored in
       the bell-ringer's body. Describe the sequence of the main energy transfers
       involved when a person rings a church bell.

       ....

       ....

       ....

       ....

3 marks

Maximum 8 marks

5. Yew Fai and Helen investigated the energy values of five different brands of cornflakes using the method shown below. They measured the increase in temperature of the water for each brand of cornflakes.

Their results are shown in the table on the right.

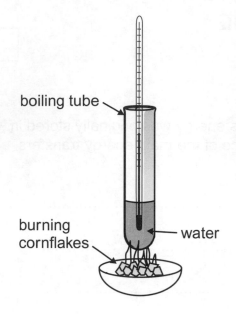

brand	starting temperature (°C)	final temperature (°C)	temperature change (°C)
A	21	41	
B	19	43	
C	20	49	
D	21	42	
E	22	50	

boiling tube

burning cornflakes — water

(a) Fill in the temperature change (°C) column of the table.

2 marks

(b) Give two things that Yew Fai and Helen needed to do to make this a fair test.

1. ....

2. ....

2 marks

(c) What could they do to improve the reliability of their results?

....

1 mark

(d) Suggest one change they could make to their apparatus to improve the accuracy of the results.

....

1 mark

Maximum 6 marks

6. Wine is about 10% alcohol and 90% water. The table shows some information about water and alcohol, and the diagram shows the equipment used to turn wine into brandy.

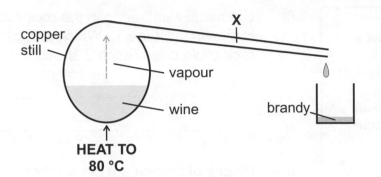

Substance	Boiling Temp.
Water	100 °C
Alcohol	78 °C

(a) What is the name of this separation process?

....

1 mark

(b) Why can you separate water and alcohol using this process?

....

1 mark

(c) What process is taking place at point X on the diagram?

....

1 mark

(d) Which do you think contains a greater percentage of alcohol, wine or brandy? Explain how you can tell from the method shown above.

....

....

....

2 marks

Maximum 5 marks

7. An igneous rock, for example granite, can become a sedimentary rock. A model of the process was carried out in a school laboratory as shown below.

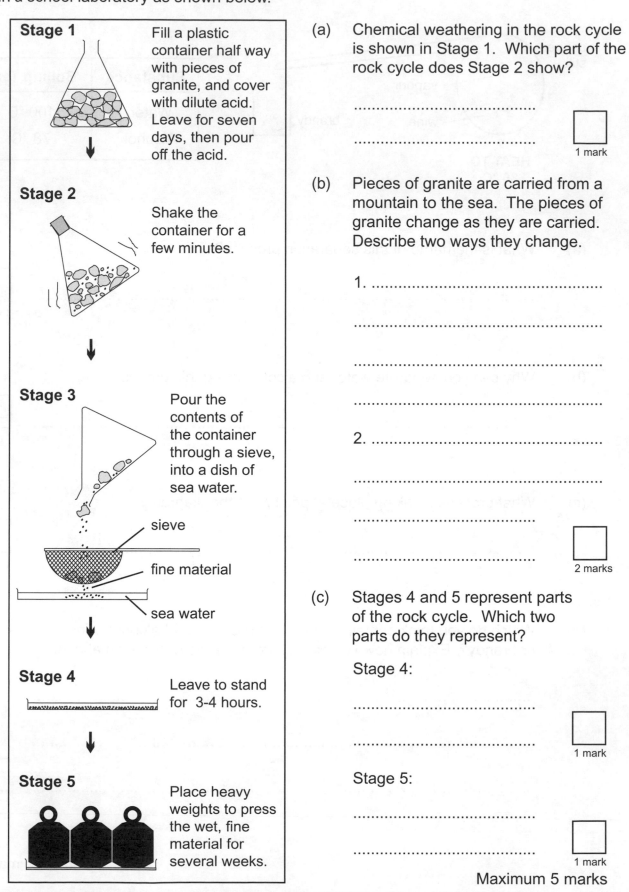

Stage 1 Fill a plastic container half way with pieces of granite, and cover with dilute acid. Leave for seven days, then pour off the acid.

Stage 2 Shake the container for a few minutes.

Stage 3 Pour the contents of the container through a sieve, into a dish of sea water.

sieve

fine material

sea water

Stage 4 Leave to stand for 3-4 hours.

Stage 5 Place heavy weights to press the wet, fine material for several weeks.

(a) Chemical weathering in the rock cycle is shown in Stage 1. Which part of the rock cycle does Stage 2 show?

....

....

☐ 1 mark

(b) Pieces of granite are carried from a mountain to the sea. The pieces of granite change as they are carried. Describe two ways they change.

1. ....

....

....

....

2. ....

....

....

☐ 2 marks

(c) Stages 4 and 5 represent parts of the rock cycle. Which two parts do they represent?

Stage 4:

....

....

☐ 1 mark

Stage 5:

....

....

☐ 1 mark

Maximum 5 marks

8. Mr Grey likes making toast in front of his open fire.

(a) He made his toasting fork himself. He had a choice of these materials:

copper   **steel**   **plastic**   **wood**

Suggest a good choice of material for:

(i) The handle. ....

Give a reason for your choice.

....

2 marks

(ii) The prongs. ....

Give a reason for your choice.

....

2 marks

(b) Smoke from his fire always goes up the chimney.
Explain why this happens.

....

....

1 mark

(c) Explain how energy gets from the fire to the slice of toast.

....

....

1 mark

Maximum 6 marks

9. Libby investigated the chemical reaction between sulfur powder and iron filings.
She mixed them together in a crucible and heated them strongly in a Bunsen flame
for five minutes.

She recorded her observations in the table below.

Substance	Description	Appearance	Magnetic?
1	Iron filings	Grey filings	Yes
2	Sulfur powder	Yellow powder	No
3	Mixture	Yellow and grey powder	Grey bits only
4	Final product	Shiny black solid	No

(a) Write down one safety precaution Libby will need to take in this investigation.

....

1 mark

(b) Write down the substance number of one element and one compound
from the table above.

Element: ....   Compound: ....

2 marks

(c) (i) Write down the **name** of the substance produced
in the chemical reaction.

....

1 mark

(ii) When iron (Fe) and sulfur (S) atoms join together, one atom of
iron combines with one atom of sulfur.
Write down the **chemical formula** of the substance produced.

....

1 mark

(d) Libby began the experiment with 5.6 g iron and reacted it all with sulfur.
Tick the box you think is the most likely mass of the product.

☐ 5.6 g   ☐ 2.8 g   ☐ 8.8 g   ☐ 1.0 g

1 mark

Maximum 6 marks

10. A candle burns under a glass jar.

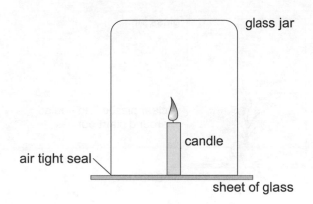

glass jar

candle

air tight seal

sheet of glass

(a) (i) There is a reaction when the candle burns.
Give the chemical formulae of two of the products of this reaction.

1. ....

2. ....

2 marks

(ii) What could you see to show that a chemical reaction
is taking place? Give two examples.

1. ....

....

2. ....

....

2 marks

Continued over the page

(b)   The candle is replaced with a pot plant.

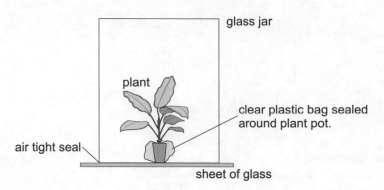

(i)   What effect does the plant's photosynthesis have on
       the levels of different gases in the jar?

       1. ....

       2. ....

                                                                        2 marks

(ii)   If you covered the jar with a black bag, what effect
       would this have on these changes?

       ....

       ....

       ....

                                                                        2 marks

(c)   Plants need chlorophyll to photosynthesise.

(i)   Which part of the cell contains chlorophyll?

       ....

                                                                        1 mark

(ii)   Which part of the cell controls chlorophyll production?

       ....

                                                                        1 mark

Maximum 10 marks

11. Wind power can be used to generate electricity using wind turbines like the one below.

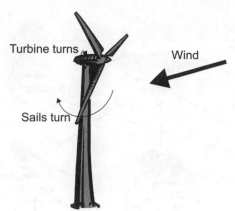

Turbine turns

Wind

Sails turn

(a) As the wind spins the sails of the wind turbine, it turns a generator, which produces electricity.
Describe the useful energy transfers which take place in this process.

....

....

....

....

2 marks

(b) Explain why wind is called a renewable energy resource.

....

....

1 mark

(c) Give one further example of a renewable energy resource that can be used to generate electricity.

....

1 marks

Maximum 4 marks

12. The diagram below shows a food web.

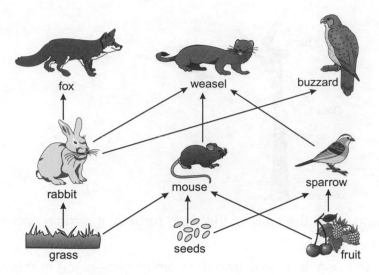

(a) Name two primary consumers from this food web.

.... 2 marks

(b) Name two secondary consumers from this food web.

.... 2 marks

(c) What is the source of energy for all food webs?

.... 1 mark

(d) If all the rabbits were killed by a disease, what do you think
would happen to the populations of the following animals?
Give a reason for your answer in each case.

   (i) the weasels?

   ....

   .... 1 mark

   (ii) the mice?

   ....

   .... 1 mark

Maximum 7 marks

13. Mrs Lightfoot and her elephant walk across a wooden floor.
Mrs Lightfoot's high heels leave marks on the floor. The elephant's feet do not.

The elephant has a mass of 3000 kg. Mrs Lightfoot has a mass of 50 kg.

Explain why Mrs Lightfoot's heels mark the floor
but the elephant does no damage.

....

....

2 marks

Maximum 2 marks

14. Sid makes a stack of 800 kg of bricks on top of a board.
The board has an area of 0.25 square metres.

(a) Work out the weight of the bricks in newtons (g = 10 N/kg).

....

1 mark

(b) Calculate the pressure under the board.

....

....

....

2 marks

Maximum 3 marks

END OF TEST

Key Stage 3

Science Test

Practice Paper 3B

Science

KEY STAGE
3

PRACTICE PAPER
3B

Read this page, but don't open the booklet until your teacher says you can start. Write your name and school in the spaces below.

First Name _____

Last Name _____

School _____

Remember

- You have one hour to do the paper.

- Make sure you have these things with you before you start: pen, pencil, rubber, ruler, angle measurer or protractor, calculator.

- The easier questions are at the start of the paper.

- Try to answer all of the questions.

- Don't use any rough paper — write all your answers and working in this test paper.

- Check your work carefully.

- If you're not sure what to do, ask your teacher.

1. Some friends are having a tug of war. The diagram shows the two teams and the force with which each person is pulling.

27 N 24 N 21 N   19 N   32 N   23 N

TEAM A   TEAM B

Which team will win, if each person pulls with a constant force?
Show your working.

....

....

....

3 marks

Maximum 3 marks

2. Alcohol is a recreational drug.

(a) Which one of these properties makes alcohol a **drug**?
Circle the correct answer.

It's a
chemical.

It can provide
energy.

It's soluble in
water.

It affects the
nervous system.

☐ 1 mark

(b) Look at this graph:

(i) Use the graph to describe how an increase in the amount of alcohol in the blood affects a person's chance of having an accident.

....

....

....

☐ 2 marks

(ii) Which of the following could explain why alcohol in the blood could cause accidents? Circle the correct answer.

Alcohol lowers body
temperature.

Alcohol is a stimulant.

Alcohol increases
the time it takes for
a person to react.

Alcohol makes
people happy.

☐ 1 mark

Maximum 4 marks

3. The diagram shows a sketch of a cell from a rabbit as seen down a powerful microscope.

(a)   Label the diagram:

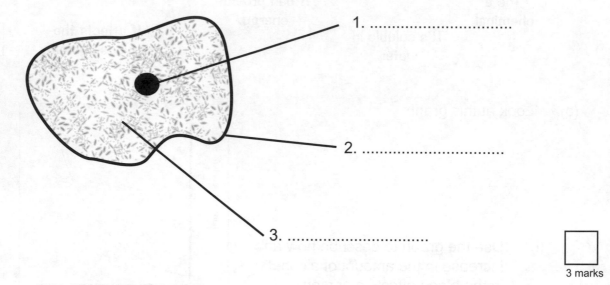

1. ....

2. ....

3. ....

3 marks

(b)   Name two parts which would be found in a plant cell and not in an animal one.

1. ....

2. ....

2 marks

(c)   The cell is one of a group of similar cells working together.
What is such a group of similar cells called?

....

1 mark

Maximum 6 marks

4. Use the information in the table below to answer the questions that follow.

SUBSTANCE	CHEMICAL FORMULA
water	H_2O
carbon dioxide	CO_2
alcohol (ethanol)	C_2H_5OH
glucose	$C_6H_{12}O_6$
oxygen	O_2

(a) Which substance is an element?

....

1 mark

(b) Which element is present in all the substances?

....

1 mark

(c) How many atoms are there in one molecule of glucose?

....

1 mark

Maximum 3 marks

5. Wayne is investigating friction in liquids. He times how long it takes a marble to fall through a tube filled with wallpaper paste.

Here are his results:

Distance fallen by marble (cm)	Time taken (s)
10	2.1
20	4.3
30	6.0
40	8.4
50	9.9

(a) Use the blank graph paper below to draw a graph of Wayne's results. Draw a line of best fit.

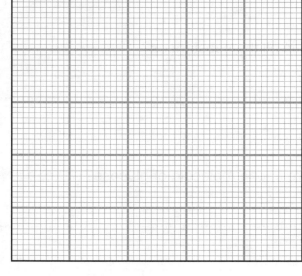

Time taken (s)

3 marks

(b) What do his results tell Wayne about the speed of the falling marble?

....

....

1 mark

Maximum 4 marks

6. A general equation for a neutralisation reaction is:

acid + alkali → a salt + water

(a) Draw lines to connect each of the salts below to the acid and the alkali that would react to form them.

Acid	Salt	Alkali
hydrochloric acid	calcium chloride	copper hydroxide
sulfuric acid	iron nitrate	calcium hydroxide
nitric acid	copper sulfate	iron hydroxide

3 marks

(b) Complete the word equation for the following neutralisation reaction:

sodium hydroxide + ... → sodium chloride + water

1 mark

(c) Write down the name of the acid that has the chemical formula: HNO_3.

....

1 mark

Maximum 5 marks

7. Matt uses a pump to inflate a balloon.
He notices that the pump gets hot as he uses it.

(a) Energy was transferred by pumping up the balloon.
Give the energy store that the energy was transferred from and the energy store of the gas that it was transferred to.

....

.... ☐

2 marks

(b) Explain how the gas molecules inside the balloon exert pressure on the walls of the balloon.

....

.... ☐

1 mark

(c) The air going into the balloon is warmed up by the pumping.
How will this affect the motion of the gas molecules inside the balloon?

....

.... ☐

1 mark

(d) As the air in the balloon becomes hotter, the pressure rises. Write down one reason, in terms of the motion of gas molecules, why the pressure rises.

....

.... ☐

1 mark

Maximum 5 marks

8. Methane is a gas. A molecule of methane consists of one carbon atom chemically joined to four hydrogen atoms.

(a) Write a word equation for the reaction that happens when methane burns in air.

.... 2 marks

(b) If pure methane is burnt in a closed container, how will the air inside the container be different afterwards? Tick any answers that apply.

The air inside the container will contain:

☐ More hydrogen   ☐ More oxygen

☐ More carbon dioxide   ☐ More sulfur dioxide

☐ Less hydrogen   ☐ Less oxygen

☐ Less carbon dioxide   ☐ Less sulfur dioxide

2 marks

(c) When methane was burnt in a closed container, carbon (soot) and carbon monoxide were formed, as well as the usual products.
Which of the following is the best explanation for this?

A   The methane burned too quickly.

B   The air inside the container was too damp.

C   There was not enough oxygen for the methane to burn completely.

D   The methane contained impurities.

Answer: ....

1 mark

Maximum 5 marks

9. The diagram shows a plank pivoted at one end.
A force of 100 N pushes up on the plank.

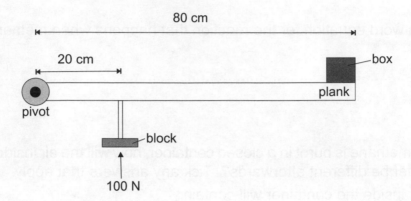

(a) Calculate the moment (turning affect) of the 100 N force about the pivot.
Show your working.

....

....

3 marks

(b) The box is on the right hand end of the plank.
It is just heavy enough to keep the plank balanced.

(i) What is the moment of the box about the pivot? Give the units.

....

1 mark

(ii) What is the weight of the box?

....

1 mark

(iii) The 100 N force acts on a block with area 5 cm².
Calculate the pressure on the block. Give the units.

....

....

....

....

2 marks

Maximum 7 marks

10. Tony is carrying out an experiment to compare the rate of photosynthesis of two types of algae. The following diagram shows the reaction that happens.

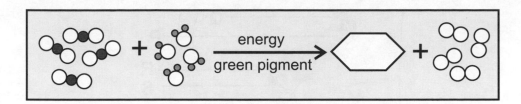

(a)   Write out the word equation for this reaction.

....

1 mark

The diagram shows the equipment Tony is using for the experiment.

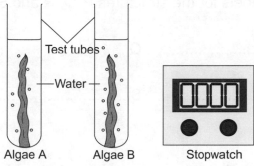

Test tubes

Water

Algae A   Algae B   Stopwatch

(b)   How can Tony use this equipment to measure the rate of photosynthesis?

....

1 mark

(c)   What can Tony do to make his results reliable?

....

1 mark

(d)   Name the green pigment needed for photosynthesis to happen.

....

1 mark

(e)   How is energy transferred to the algae to drive this reaction?

....

1 mark

Maximum 5 marks

11. The diagram shows the human female reproductive system.

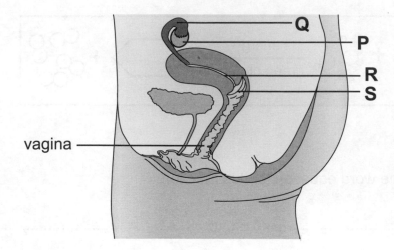

(a) Give the correct labels for the structures P, Q, R and S.

P .... Q ....

R .... S ....

4 marks

(b) From which part are the ova or eggs released at ovulation?

....

1 mark

(c) On approximately which day in the menstrual cycle does ovulation occur (if day one is when menstruation begins)?

....

1 mark

(d) Explain how the uterus changes each month to prepare for a fertilised egg.

....

1 mark

Maximum 7 marks

12. In an experiment, a ray of sunlight was directed onto a triangular prism made out of glass, as shown below.

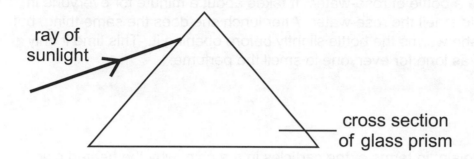

ray of sunlight

cross section of glass prism

(a) Complete the diagram to show what happens to the ray of light.

3 marks

(b) Which of the following words correctly describe what happens to the ray of light? Tick **two** boxes.

☐ absorption

☐ dispersion

☐ refraction

☐ radiation

2 marks

Maximum 5 marks

13. A teacher shows her class two different experiments. She pushes a metal coin through a slot into a money box.

Next, she takes the coin out and heats it strongly. She tries to put the heated coin into the money box, but it won't fit through the slot.

In her second experiment, the teacher stands at the end of the classroom and opens a bottle of rose-water. It takes about a minute for everyone in the class to smell the rose-water. After lunch she does the same thing, but this time she warms the bottle slightly before opening it. This time it only takes half as long for everyone to smell the perfume.

(a) Explain, in terms of the particles in the coin, why the heated coin won't fit through the slot.

....

....

....

2 marks

(b) Explain, in terms of particles, why the class smelled the rose-water more quickly when it had been warmed.

....

....

....

2 marks

(c) What do both of your explanations have in common?

....

....

2 marks

Maximum 6 marks

14. Look at this circuit diagram.

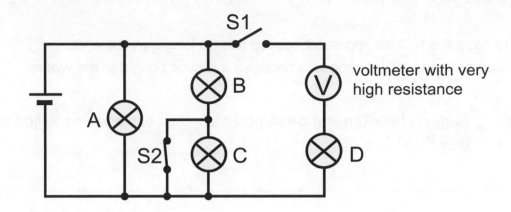

There are four bulbs, **A**, **B**, **C** and **D**, in the circuit.

(a) In the spaces below, state which bulbs are lit and which are not lit when switch S1 is open and S2 is closed as shown above.

Lit bulbs ....

Unlit bulbs ....

2 marks

(b) What three changes should be made to the circuit shown above to make sure all the bulbs are lit?

1. ....

2. ....

3. ....

3 marks

Maximum 5 marks

15. Potassium chloride is a white, crystalline solid at room temperature. Tim and Sarah are carrying out an experiment to see what happens when they mix potassium chloride crystals (KCl) with water. They add some KCl crystals to a beaker of water and stir it.

Tim says the KCl disappears because it is no longer in the water.
Sarah says the KCl disappears because it has dissolved in the water.

(a) Suggest how Tim and Sarah could test their explanations to find out who is right.

....

....

2 marks

Sarah suggests testing their explanations by putting a piece of magnesium into the beaker. She says that the potassium will leave a deposit on the magnesium as they react. They try this, but there is no reaction.

Tim says the lack of a reaction proves there was no KCl in the solution.
Sarah is confused because her textbook says that KCl dissolves in water.

(b) Use the data below to explain why Tim is wrong.

....

1 mark

> **Reactivity Series**
>
> Potassium
> Sodium
> Calcium
> Magnesium
> Aluminium

(c) Would it be better for Sarah and Tim to rely on their first-hand experience or a secondary source? Give a reason for your answer.

....

....

2 marks

Maximum 5 marks

END OF TEST

Key Stage 3

English Test

Reading Paper
Vampires
Set A

Read this page, but don't open the booklet until your teacher says you can start. Write your name and school in the spaces below.

First Name _____

Last Name _____

School _____

Instructions

■ Before you start to write, you have **15 minutes** to read the Reading Booklet.

■ From that point you will have **1 hour** to write your answers.

■ Try to answer **all** of the questions.

■ There are **14** questions, worth **32 marks**.

■ Check through all of your work carefully before the end of the test.

■ If you're not sure what to do, ask your teacher.

Questions 1-5 are about *Yikes! Vampire Bats Can Run, Too*
(pages 3-4 in the Reading Booklet)

1. From the first paragraph of the article, write down three things a vampire bat can do.

    •......................................   •......................................   •......................................

2. How does the title of the article grab the reader's attention? Explain one way.

    ....

    ....

3. Look at paragraphs 5 and 6. Explain one way in which the writer links these paragraphs together smoothly. Support your answer with a quotation.

    ....

    ....

    ....

4. a) From the first three paragraphs, write down a phrase which tells the reader that vampire bats can be quite fast.

        ....

    b) Write down a word from the section "On to the treadmill" which suggests that cattle move slowly.

        ....

5. In the whole article, how does the writer try to make the information entertaining and easy to understand for the reader?

You should comment on:
- the way the article is organised;
- the writer's use of informal language;
- the comparisons the writer uses.

....

....

....

....

....

....

....

....

....

....

....

....

....

5 marks

6.   Look at paragraph 1. Give one way in which the writer makes the opening of the article interesting for a teenage audience.

....

1 mark

7.   Give one reason from paragraph 4 why Darren Shan thinks that "Cirque Du Freak" is *not* a reckless or irresponsible book.

....

....

1 mark

8.   In paragraph 5, what two elements does Darren Shan argue are needed for a good horror story?

....

....

....

2 marks

9. Explain how the whole article shows the author Darren Shan's enthusiasm for horror stories.

You should comment on:
- the language he uses to describe his own reactions to horror stories;
- the effects of the range of punctuation he uses;
- the way he writes about how a reader of horror stories should be affected.

....

....

....

....

....

....

....

....

....

....

....

....

....

....

5 marks

10. Give one detail in paragraph 1 that tells us that it is night-time.

....

11. In the first 10 lines of paragraph 1, the narrator tells the reader how he feels about being in Count Dracula's castle. Pick out two phrases or sentences and explain what each one suggests about the narrator's feelings.
Write your answers in the table below.

Words from the text	What they suggest

☐ 2 marks

12. The narrator's feelings change between the middle of paragraph 1 and the middle of paragraph 2.

a)   Describe the narrator's feelings in the middle of paragraph 1.
        Support your answer with a quotation.

        ....

        ....

b)   Describe the narrator's feelings by the middle of paragraph 2.
        Support your answer with a quotation.

        ....

        ....

4 marks

13.   In the last paragraph, the narrator repeats certain words. Pick out one
        example of repetition. Explain what it suggests to the reader about the
        narrator's state of mind.

        Example

        ....

        ....

        What it suggests about the narrator's state of mind

        ....

        ....

1 mark

14. *Yikes! Vampire Bats Can Run Too* and *Dracula* each have a different tone and atmosphere. Complete the table below by explaining how each phrase makes the reader feel about the creature it is describing.

	Words from text	Effect on the reader
Yikes! Vampire Bats Can Run, Too	"Hopping is good, when you're a bat slurping cow blood, because cows are heavy and can kick or roll over and squash a bat"	
	"the clever little mammals dutifully kept pace"	
Dracula	"down the castle wall over the dreadful abyss, face down with his cloak spreading out around him like great wings."	
	"what manner of creature is it in the semblance of man?"	

4 marks

Key Stage 3

English Test

Writing Paper
Set A

English

KEY STAGE
3

PRACTICE PAPER
Writing
Set A

Read this page, but don't open the booklet until your teacher says you can start. Write your name and school in the spaces below.

First Name _____

Last Name _____

School _____

Instructions

☐ This paper is **1 hour and 15 minutes** long.

☐ You should spend about:

45 minutes on Section A

30 minutes on Section B

☐ Section A, the longer writing task, is worth **30 marks**.

☐ Section B, the shorter writing task, is worth **20 marks**.

☐ You should spend 15 minutes planning your answer to Section A, using the planning grid provided.

☐ Check through all of your work carefully before the end of the test.

☐ If you're not sure what to do, ask your teacher.

Section A — Longer writing task

Improving the Common Room

Spend about 45 minutes on this section.

You are a member of your school's Student Council. Earlier in the year, the Council received some money from the Parents' Association to spend on improving the Year 9 common room. You get this note from the head of the Student Council:

It's nearly the summer holidays, so I want to thank you for your help with the Student Council's work this year. I think we've achieved a lot!

There's one last job to do before we enjoy that well earned rest. Do you remember that, earlier in the year, the Parents' Association gave us £100 to spend on the common room? Well, they're having a meeting soon and I need someone to write a formal report for them on how we spent the money. The report needs to explain what we've done, how it's improved things and what else still needs doing.

Could you do this for me please?
Thanks!

Write a report for the Parents' Association, explaining how the Student Council have spent the £100 on improving the Year 9 common room and what improvements are needed in the future.

(30 marks)

Use this page to plan your work.

This page will not be marked.

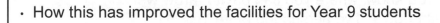

· Details of what you spent the money on and why

· How this has improved the facilities for Year 9 students

· What improvements are still needed in the common room and why

Section B — Shorter writing task

Summer Fair Fundraising

Spend about 30 minutes on this section.

You are helping to organise your school's summer fair. You receive this note from one of the other organisers:

> Hi! How's it going?
>
> I'm hoping we can raise over £1,000 this year — which would beat last year's target by £200. Since all profits go to charity, it's worth a try.
>
> I'm having trouble getting enough volunteers for the stocks — you know, where you can pay to throw wet sponges at people. I've persuaded three Year 11 students to volunteer, but no teachers have yet.
>
> Could you write a couple of paragraphs for the staff newsletter to try to persuade some of them to volunteer? You can keep it quite light-hearted.
> It would only be for ½ hour each, the sponges would be soaked in WARM water — and it is for charity!

Write a short article for the staff newsletter to persuade teachers to volunteer for a turn in the stocks at this year's summer fair.

(20 marks including 4 for spelling)

Key Stage 3

English Test

Shakespeare Paper
Romeo and Juliet

Set A

English

KEY STAGE
3

PRACTICE PAPER
Shakespeare
Set A

Read this page, but don't open the booklet until your teacher says you can start. Write your name and school in the spaces below.

First Name _____

Last Name _____

School _____

Instructions

- This test is **45 minutes** long.

- You will be tested on your reading and understanding of *Romeo and Juliet*. There are **18 marks** for this paper.

- Check through all of your work carefully before the end of the test.

- If you're not sure what to do, ask your teacher.

Romeo and Juliet
Act 1 Scene 1, lines 98 to 176
Act 2 Scene 2, lines 25 to 78

In the first extract, Montague wants to know why his servants have been fighting, and why Romeo is so sad. In the second, Romeo and Juliet talk about what is stopping them from being together.

What do you learn about different characters' attitudes to love and family honour in these extracts?

Support your ideas by referring to both of the extracts which are printed on the following pages.

(18 marks)

Romeo and Juliet
Act 1 Scene 1, lines 98 to 176

> In this extract, Montague asks Benvolio why his servants have been quarrelling.
> The Montagues also say that their son Romeo is sad. Benvolio decides to find out why.

All exit, except MONTAGUE, LADY MONTAGUE, *and* BENVOLIO.

MONTAGUE	Who set this ancient quarrel new abroach?	
	Speak, nephew, were you by when it began?	
BENVOLIO	Here were the servants of your adversary,	100
	And yours, close fighting ere I did approach:	
	I drew to part them — in the instant came	
	The fiery Tybalt, with his sword prepared,	
	Which, as he breathed defiance to my ears,	
	He swung about his head and cut the winds,	105
	Who nothing hurt withal hissed him in scorn:	
	While we were interchanging thrusts and blows,	
	Came more and more and fought on part and part,	
	Till the Prince came, who parted either part.	
LADY MONTAGUE	O, where is Romeo? Saw you him today?	110
	Right glad I am he was not at this fray.	
BENVOLIO	Madam, an hour before the worshipped sun	
	Peered forth the golden window of the east,	
	A troubled mind drove me to walk abroad,	
	Where, underneath the grove of sycamore	115
	That westward rooteth from the city side,	
	So early walking did I see your son.	
	Towards him I made, but he was ware of me,	
	And stole into the covert of the wood:	
	I, measuring his affections by my own,	120
	Which then most sought where most might not be found,	
	Being one too many by my weary self,	
	Pursued my humour, not pursuing his,	
	And gladly shunned who gladly fled from me.	
MONTAGUE	Many a morning hath he there been seen,	125
	With tears augmenting the fresh morning's dew.	

Adding to clouds more clouds with his deep sighs;
But all so soon as the all-cheering sun
Should in the farthest east begin to draw
The shady curtains from Aurora's bed,   130
Away from light steals home my heavy son,
And private in his chamber pens himself,
Shuts up his windows, locks fair daylight out,
And makes himself an artificial night:
Black and portentous must this humour prove,   135
Unless good counsel may the cause remove.

BENVOLIO	My noble uncle, do you know the cause?
MONTAGUE	I neither know it, nor can learn of him.
BENVOLIO	Have you importuned him by any means?

MONTAGUE   Both by myself and many other friends: 140
But he, his own affections' counsellor,
Is to himself — I will not say how true —
But to himself so secret and so close,
So far from sounding and discovery,
As is the bud bit with an envious worm,   145
Ere he can spread his sweet leaves to the air,
Or dedicate his beauty to the sun.
Could we but learn from whence his sorrows grow.
We would as willingly give cure as know.

Enter ROMEO

BENVOLIO   See, where he comes. So please you, step aside;   150
I'll know his grievance, or be much denied.

MONTAGUE   I would thou wert so happy by thy stay,
To hear true shrift. Come, madam, let's away.

Exit MONTAGUE and LADY MONTAGUE

BENVOLIO	Good morrow, cousin.
ROMEO	Is the day so young?
BENVOLIO	But new struck nine.

ROMEO   Ay me! Sad hours seem long. 155
Was that my father that went hence so fast?

BENVOLIO	It was. What sadness lengthens Romeo's hours?
ROMEO	Not having that, which, having, makes them short.
BENVOLIO	In love?

ROMEO	Out —	160
BENVOLIO	Of love?	
ROMEO	Out of her favour where I am in love.	
BENVOLIO	Alas that love so gentle in his view, Should be so tyrannous and rough in proof!	
ROMEO	Alas, that Love, whose view is muffled still, Should, without eyes, see pathways to his will! Where shall we dine? O me! What fray was here? Yet tell me not, for I have heard it all. Here's much to do with hate, but more with love. Why, then, O brawling love, O loving hate, O anything, of nothing first create! O heavy lightness, serious vanity, Misshapen chaos of well-seeming forms! Feather of lead, bright smoke, cold fire, sick health! Still-waking sleep, that is not what it is! This love feel I, that feel no love in this.	165 170 175

Act 2 Scene 2, lines 25 to 78

> In this extract, Romeo talks to Juliet at her balcony,
> and they both promise to give up their family names for love.

JULIET	Ay me!	
ROMEO (*Aside*)	She speaks.	25
	O speak again, bright angel, for thou art As glorious to this night, being o'er my head, As is a wingèd messenger of heaven Unto the white-upturnèd wondering eyes Of mortals that fall back to gaze on him, When he bestrides the lazy-passing clouds, And sails upon the bosom of the air.	 30
JULIET	O Romeo, Romeo, wherefore art thou Romeo? Deny thy father and refuse thy name. Or if thou wilt not, be but sworn my love, And I'll no longer be a Capulet.	 35
ROMEO (*Aside*)	Shall I hear more, or shall I speak at this?	
JULIET	'Tis but thy name that is my enemy — Thou art thyself, though not a Montague. What's Montague? It is nor hand nor foot, Nor arm nor face, nor any other part Belonging to a man. O be some other name!	 40

What's in a name? That which we call a rose
By any other word would smell as sweet;
So Romeo would, were he not Romeo called,   45
Retain that dear perfection which he owes
Without that title. Romeo, doff thy name,
And for thy name, which is no part of thee,
Take all myself.

ROMEO   I take thee at thy word.
Call me but love, and I'll be new baptised;   50
Henceforth I never will be Romeo.

JULIET   What man art thou that thus bescreened in night
So stumblest on my counsel?

ROMEO   By a name
I know not how to tell thee who I am.
My name, dear saint, is hateful to myself,   55
Because it is an enemy to thee;
Had I it written, I would tear the word.

JULIET   My ears have yet not drunk a hundred words
Of thy tongue's uttering, yet I know the sound.
Art thou not Romeo, and a Montague?   60

ROMEO   Neither, fair maid, if either thee dislike.

JULIET   How camest thou hither, tell me, and wherefore?
The orchard walls are high and hard to climb,
And the place death, considering who thou art,
If any of my kinsmen find thee here.   65

ROMEO   With love's light wings did I o'erperch these walls,
For stony limits cannot hold love out,
And what love can do, that dares love attempt:
Therefore thy kinsmen are no stop to me.

JULIET   If they do see thee, they will murder thee.   70

ROMEO   Alack, there lies more peril in thine eye
Than twenty of their swords. Look thou but sweet,
And I am proof against their enmity.

JULIET   I would not for the world they saw thee here.

ROMEO   I have night's cloak to hide me from their eyes,   75
And but thou love me, let them find me here.
My life were better ended by their hate,
Than death proroguèd, wanting of thy love.

END OF TEST

Key Stage 3

English Test

Shakespeare Paper
The Tempest
Set A

English

KEY STAGE
3

PRACTICE PAPER
Shakespeare
Set A

Read this page, but don't open the booklet until your teacher says you can start. Write your name and school in the spaces below.

First Name _____

Last Name _____

School _____

Instructions

- This test is **45 minutes** long.

- You will be tested on your reading and understanding of *The Tempest*. There are **18 marks** for this paper.

- Check through all of your work carefully before the end of the test.

- If you're not sure what to do, ask your teacher.

The Tempest
Act 1 Scene 2, lines 390 to 453
Act 3 Scene 1, lines 37 to 91

In the first extract, Ferdinand has just been shipwrecked
and is led away by Ariel to meet Miranda. In the second,
Ferdinand and Miranda promise to marry each other.

**In these extracts, how does Ferdinand's language show
how he is feeling?**

*Support your ideas by referring to both of the extracts which
are printed on the following pages.*

(18 marks)

The Tempest
Act 1 Scene 2, lines 390 to 453

In this extract, Ferdinand meets Miranda for the first time and instantly falls in love with her. He wants to impress her but he is still sad about the death of his father.

FERDINAND	Where should this music be? I' th' air or th' earth?	390
	It sounds no more, and sure it waits upon	
	Some god o' th' island. Sitting on a bank,	
	Weeping again the King my father's wreck,	
	This music crept by me upon the waters,	
	Allaying both their fury and my passion	395
	With its sweet air. Thence I have followed it,	
	Or it hath drawn me rather. But 'tis gone.	
	No, it begins again.	
ARIEL (*Sings*)	Full fathom five thy father lies;	
	Of his bones are coral made;	400
	Those are pearls that were his eyes;	
	Nothing of him that doth fade	
	But doth suffer a sea-change	
	Into something rich and strange.	
	Sea-nymphs hourly ring his knell:	405
SPIRITS	Ding-dong.	
ARIEL	Hark! Now I hear them.	
ARIEL and SPIRITS	Ding dong bell.	
FERDINAND	The ditty does remember my drowned father.	
	This is no mortal business, nor no sound	410
	That the earth owes. I hear it now above me.	
PROSPERO (*To* MIRANDA)	The fringed curtains of thine eye advance,	
	And say what thou seest yond.	
MIRANDA	What is't? A spirit?	
	Lord, how it looks about! Believe me, sir,	
	It carries a brave form. But 'tis a spirit.	415
PROSPERO	No, wench — it eats and sleeps and hath such senses	
	As we have, such. This gallant which thou seest	
	Was in the wreck, and but he's something stained	
	With grief, that's beauty's canker, thou mightst call him	
	A goodly person. He hath lost his fellows,	420
	And strays about to find 'em.	
MIRANDA	I might call him	
	A thing divine, for nothing natural	
	I ever saw so noble.	

PROSPERO (*Aside*)   It goes on, I see,
          As my soul prompts it. Spirit, fine spirit! I'll free thee
          Within two days for this.

FERDINAND (*Seeing* MIRANDA)   Most sure, the goddess   425
          On whom these airs attend! Vouchsafe my pray'r
          May know if you remain upon this island,
          And that you will some good instruction give
          How I may bear me here. My prime request,
          Which I do last pronounce, is — O you wonder! —   430
          If you be maid or no?

MIRANDA   No wonder, sir —
          But certainly a maid.

FERDINAND   My language? Heavens!
          I am the best of them that speak this speech,
          Were I but where 'tis spoken.

PROSPERO   How the best?
          What wert thou, if the King of Naples heard thee?   435

FERDINAND   A single thing, as I am now, that wonders
          To hear thee speak of Naples. He does hear me,
          And that he does I weep. Myself am Naples,
          Who with mine eyes, never since at ebb, beheld
          The King my father wrecked.

MIRANDA   Alack, for mercy!   440

FERDINAND   Yes, faith, and all his lords, the Duke of Milan
          And his brave son being twain.

PROSPERO (*Aside*)   The Duke of Milan
          And his more braver daughter could control thee,
          If now 'twere fit to do't. At the first sight
          They have changed eyes. Delicate Ariel,   445
          I'll set thee free for this. (*To* FERDINAND) A word,
                              good sir —
          I fear you have done yourself some wrong — a word.

MIRANDA (*Aside*) Why speaks my father so ungently? This
          Is the third man that e'er I saw, the first
          That e'er I sighed for. Pity move my father   450
          To be inclined my way!

FERDINAND   O, if a virgin,
          And your affection not gone forth, I'll make you
          The Queen of Naples.

Act 3 Scene 1, lines 37 to 91

> In this extract, Ferdinand works hard to complete the task
> Prospero has set him. He talks to Miranda about his feelings for
> her and they promise to get married.

FERDINAND   Admired Miranda!
          Indeed the top of admiration, worth
          What's dearest to the world! Full many a lady
          I have eyed with best regard, and many a time   40
          Th' harmony of their tongues hath into bondage
          Brought my too diligent ear. For several virtues
          Have I liked several women, never any
          With so full soul, but some defect in her
          Did quarrel with the noblest grace she owed,   45
          And put it to the foil — but you, O you,
          So perfect and so peerless, are created
          Of every creature's best!

MIRANDA   I do not know
          One of my sex, no woman's face remember,
          Save, from my glass, mine own, nor have I seen   50
          More that I may call men than you, good friend,
          And my dear father. How features are abroad,
          I am skilless of, but, by my modesty,
          The jewel in my dower, I would not wish
          Any companion in the world but you,   55
          Nor can imagination form a shape,
          Besides yourself, to like of. But I prattle
          Something too wildly, and my father's precepts
          I therein do forget.

FERDINAND   I am, in my condition,
          A prince, Miranda. I do think, a king —   60
          I would not so — and would no more endure
          This wooden slavery than to suffer
          The flesh-fly blow my mouth! Hear my soul speak:
          The very instant that I saw you, did
          My heart fly to your service, there resides   65
          To make me slave to it, and for your sake
          Am I this patient log-man.

MIRANDA	Do you love me?
FERDINAND	O heaven, O earth, bear witness to this sound, And crown what I profess with kind event, If I speak true! If hollowly, invert 70 What best is boded me to mischief! I, Beyond all limit of what else i' th' world, Do love, prize, honour you.
MIRANDA	I am a fool To weep at what I am glad of.
PROSPERO (*Aside*)	Fair encounter Of two most rare affections! Heavens rain grace 75 On that which breeds between 'em!
FERDINAND	Wherefore weep you?
MIRANDA	At mine unworthiness, that dare not offer What I desire to give, and much less take What I shall die to want. But this is trifling, And all the more it seeks to hide itself, 80 The bigger bulk it shows. Hence, bashful cunning, And prompt me, plain and holy innocence! I am your wife, if you will marry me, If not, I'll die your maid. To be your fellow You may deny me, but I'll be your servant, 85 Whether you will or no.
FERDINAND	(*He kneels*) My mistress, dearest, And I thus humble ever.
MIRANDA	My husband, then?
FERDINAND	Ay, with a heart as willing As bondage e'er of freedom. Here's my hand.
MIRANDA	And mine, with my heart in't. And now farewell 90 Till half an hour hence.
FERDINAND	A thousand thousand!

END OF TEST

Key Stage 3

English Test

Reading Paper
Changing Schools
Set B

English

KEY STAGE
3

PRACTICE PAPER
Reading
Set B

Read this page, but don't open the booklet until your teacher says
you can start. Write your name and school in the spaces below.

First Name _____

Last Name _____

School _____

Instructions

■ Before you start to write, you have **15 minutes**
to read the Reading Booklet.

■ From that point you will have **1 hour** to write your answers.

■ Try to answer **all** of the questions.

■ There are **13** questions, worth **32 marks**.

■ Check through all of your work carefully
before the end of the test.

■ If you're not sure what to do, ask your teacher.

**Questions 1-4 are about *Harry Potter and the Philosopher's Stone*
(pages 11-12 in the Reading Booklet)**

1. From the first paragraph, write down why it was difficult for Harry to remember where things were in his new school.

    ....

    ....

    □ 1 mark

2. a) In paragraph 2, the writer lists the ways that Peeves is unpleasant.
        Write down one phrase that shows he is unpleasant.

        ....

        □ 1 mark

    b) Explain why the list of ways Peeves is unpleasant is an effective way of describing his personality to the reader.

        ....

        ....

        □ 1 mark

3. The writer uses humour in her descriptions of the school.
    Give one example of humour and explain why it is effective.

    Example from text

    ....

    Why it is effective

    ....

    □ 2 marks

4. In the whole text, how does the writer create a magical atmosphere for Hogwarts School?

You should comment on:
- the language the writer uses;
- the unusual features of the school building and lessons;
- the descriptions of characters.

....

....

....

....

....

....

....

....

....

....

....

....

....

5 marks

Questions 5-8 are about *Starting 'big' school*
(pages 13-14 in the Reading Booklet)

5. Describe one technique the writer uses to attract the reader's attention in paragraph 1. Explain why it is effective.

....

....

....

2 marks

6. From Chenice's account, give one impression you get of the school. Support your answer with a quotation.

....

....

....

2 marks

7. Complete the table below to show how the way the article is organised makes it more useful to the reader.

How the article is organised	How this helps the reader
General introduction to changing schools	Helps the reader to understand what the students are going to talk about
Sections describing different pupils' experiences	
Headline and subheadings	

2 marks

8. What impression does the article give about what it's like to start secondary school?

You should comment on:
- the feelings described by the children;
- the language used in the introduction;
- the headmaster's comment.

....

....

....

....

....

....

....

....

....

....

....

....

....

....

5 marks

9. From paragraphs 1 and 2 what overall impression do you get of the evacuees' experience? Give one quotation to support your answer.

    ....

    ....

    ....

    2 marks

10. How do the logbook extracts suggest that the school is old-fashioned compared to today's schools? Give one example.

    ....

    1 mark

11. Why do you think the extracts from the logbook are included in the article? Suggest one reason.

    ....

    ....

    1 mark

12. Pick out three phrases from paragraph 3 that show that the school was uncomfortable for the children. Explain the effect of these phrases on the reader.

Phrase 1

....

....

Effect on Reader

....

....

Phrase 2

....

....

Effect on Reader

....

....

Phrase 3

....

....

Effect on Reader

....

....

3 marks

Question 13 is about *Harry Potter and the Philosopher's Stone* and *Wingrave School*

13. Both *Wingrave School* and *Harry Potter and the Philosopher's Stone* describe characters adapting to unusual conditions at school. However, they are very different types of text.

Complete the table below by:

• Circling what you think the purpose of each text is.

• Explaining your choices.

	Wingrave School	**Harry Potter and the Philosopher's Stone**
Purpose of the text (circle your answer)	entertaining informing persuading	entertaining informing persuading
Give a reason for your choice		

4 marks

Key Stage 3

English Test

Writing Paper
Set B

English

KEY STAGE

3

PRACTICE PAPER

Writing

Set B

Read this page, but don't open the booklet until your teacher says you can start. Write your name and school in the spaces below.

First Name _____

Last Name _____

School _____

Instructions

☐ This paper is **1 hour and 15 minutes** long.

☐ You should spend about:

 45 minutes on Section A

 30 minutes on Section B

☐ Section A, the longer writing task, is worth **30 marks**.

☐ Section B, the shorter writing task, is worth **20 marks**.

☐ You should spend 15 minutes planning your answer to Section A, using the planning grid provided.

☐ Check through all of your work carefully before the end of the test.

☐ If you're not sure what to do, ask your teacher.

Section A — Longer writing task

Teen Readers

Spend about 45 minutes on this section.

You have a Saturday job at the local library.

Your boss gives you this information:

> I would like to encourage more teenagers to use the library. Maybe we need to make the teenage book section more attractive. Or we could offer more services to teenagers — libraries are about more than books. Other libraries in the area are offering:
>
> - free internet access for school pupils
> - homework clubs
>
> Please write a report advising me about why teenagers don't like using the library at the moment and what we could do to encourage them to use the library more.

Write a report to advise your boss about why teenagers aren't using the library now, and how you think more teenagers could be encouraged to use the library in the future.

(30 marks)

Use this page to plan your work.

This page will not be marked.

· Why don't teenagers like the library at the moment?

· What could the library do to attract more teenagers?

· Why would these things attract teenagers?

Section B — Shorter writing task

Talent Contest

Spend about 30 minutes on this section.

You have volunteered to help organise the school's talent contest.
The teacher in charge gives you this note:

> Pupils entering the contest need to know what they're letting themselves in for!
>
> They need to know how long they have to perform for and the sorts of things they could do.
>
> They also need to know what time it's on, where it's being held and what they need to bring with them.

Write a leaflet informing pupils about the details of the talent contest.

(20 marks including 4 for spelling)

Key Stage 3

English Test

Shakespeare Paper
Romeo and Juliet
Set B

Read this page, but don't open the booklet until your teacher says you can start. Write your name and school in the spaces below.

First Name _____

Last Name _____

School _____

Instructions

- This test is **45 minutes** long.

- You will be tested on your reading and understanding of *Romeo and Juliet*. There are **18 marks** for this paper.

- Check through all of your work carefully before the end of the test.

- If you're not sure what to do, ask your teacher.

Romeo and Juliet
Act 1 Scene 1, lines 154 to 218
Act 2 Scene 2, lines 79 to 135

In the first extract Romeo tells Benvolio about Rosaline, a girl he loves. In the second, Romeo and Juliet say that they love each other.

How does Shakespeare use language to show strong emotions in these extracts?

Support your ideas by referring to both of the extracts which are printed on the following pages.

(18 marks)

Romeo and Juliet
Act 1 Scene 1, lines 154 to 218

In this extract, Romeo tells Benvolio about Rosaline, a girl he is in love with.

Exit MONTAGUE *and* LADY MONTAGUE

BENVOLIO	Good morrow, cousin.	
ROMEO	Is the day so young?	
BENVOLIO	But new struck nine.	
ROMEO	Ay me! Sad hours seem long.	155
	Was that my father that went hence so fast?	
BENVOLIO	It was. What sadness lengthens Romeo's hours?	
ROMEO	Not having that, which, having, makes them short.	
BENVOLIO	In love?	
ROMEO	Out —	160
BENVOLIO	Of love?	
ROMEO	Out of her favour where I am in love.	
BENVOLIO	Alas that love so gentle in his view,	
	Should be so tyrannous and rough in proof!	
ROMEO	Alas, that Love, whose view is muffled still,	165
	Should, without eyes, see pathways to his will!	
	Where shall we dine? O me! What fray was here?	
	Yet tell me not, for I have heard it all.	
	Here's much to do with hate, but more with love.	
	Why, then, O brawling love, O loving hate,	170
	O anything, of nothing first create!	
	O heavy lightness, serious vanity,	
	Misshapen chaos of well-seeming forms!	
	Feather of lead, bright smoke, cold fire, sick health!	
	Still-waking sleep, that is not what it is!	175
	This love feel I, that feel no love in this.	
	Dost thou not laugh?	
BENVOLIO	No, coz, I rather weep.	
ROMEO	Good heart, at what?	
BENVOLIO	At thy good heart's oppression.	
ROMEO	Why, such is love's transgression.	
	Griefs of mine own lie heavy in my breast,	180
	Which thou wilt propagate, to have it pressed	

With more of thine; this love that thou hast shown
Doth add more grief to too much of mine own.
Love is a smoke made with the fume of sighs,
Being purged, a fire sparkling in lovers' eyes,   185
Being vexed a sea nourished with lovers' tears:
What is it else? A madness most discreet,
A choking gall and a preserving sweet.
Farewell, my coz.

BENVOLIO   Soft! I will go along;
And if you leave me so, you do me wrong.   190

ROMEO   Tut, I have lost myself; I am not here,
This is not Romeo, he's some other where.

BENVOLIO   Tell me in sadness, who is that you love.

ROMEO   What, shall I groan and tell thee?

BENVOLIO   Groan! Why no,
But sadly tell me, who?   195

ROMEO   Bid a sick man in sadness make his will?
Ah, word ill urged to one that is so ill.
In sadness, cousin, I do love a woman.

BENVOLIO   I aimed so near, when I supposed you loved.

ROMEO   A right good mark-man! And she's fair I love.   200

BENVOLIO   A right fair mark, fair coz, is soonest hit.

ROMEO   Well, in that hit you miss: she'll not be hit
With Cupid's arrow, she hath Dian's wit;
And, in strong proof of chastity well armed,
From love's weak childish bow she lives uncharmed.   205
She will not stay the siege of loving terms,
Nor bide th'encounter of assailing eyes,
Nor ope her lap to saint-seducing gold:
O, she is rich in beauty, only poor,
That when she dies with beauty dies her store.   210

BENVOLIO   Then she hath sworn that she will still live chaste?

ROMEO   She hath, and in that sparing makes huge waste,
For beauty starved with her severity
Cuts beauty off from all posterity.
She is too fair, too wise, wisely too fair,   215
To merit bliss by making me despair:
She hath forsworn to love, and in that vow
Do I live dead that live to tell it now.

Act 2 Scene 2, lines 79 to 135

In this extract, Juliet talks to Romeo from her balcony.

JULIET   By whose direction found'st thou out this place?

ROMEO   By Love, that first did prompt me to enquire: 80
              He lent me counsel, and I lent him eyes.
              I am no pilot, yet wert thou as far
              As that vast shore washed with the farthest sea,
              I should adventure for such merchandise.

JULIET   Thou knowest the mask of night is on my face,   85
              Else would a maiden blush bepaint my cheek
              For that which thou hast heard me speak tonight.
              Fain would I dwell on form, fain, fain deny
              What I have spoke, but farewell compliment.
              Dost thou love me? I know thou wilt say 'Ay',   90
              And I will take thy word; yet if thou swear'st,
              Thou mayst prove false: at lovers' perjuries
              They say Jove laughs. O gentle Romeo,
              If thou dost love, pronounce it faithfully.
              Or if thou think'st I am too quickly won,   95
              I'll frown and be perverse, and say thee nay,
              So thou wilt woo, but else not for the world.
              In truth, fair Montague, I am too fond,
              And therefore thou mayst think my behaviour light:
              But trust me, gentleman, I'll prove more true   100
              Than those that have more cunning to be strange.
              I should have been more strange, I must confess,
              But that thou overheard'st, ere I was ware,
              My true-love passion — therefore pardon me,
              And not impute this yielding to light love,   105
              Which the dark night hath so discoverèd.

ROMEO   Lady, by yonder blessèd moon I vow,
              That tips with silver all these fruit-tree tops —

JULIET   O swear not by the moon, th'inconstant moon,
              That monthly changes in her circled orb,   110
              Lest that thy love prove likewise variable.

ROMEO	What shall I swear by?
JULIET	Do not swear at all.
	Or if thou wilt, swear by thy gracious self,
	Which is the god of my idolatry,
	And I'll believe thee.

ROMEO	If my heart's dear love —	115

JULIET	Well, do not swear. Although I joy in thee,
	I have no joy of this contract tonight,
	It is too rash, too unadvised, too sudden,
	Too like the lightning, which doth cease to be
	Ere one can say 'It lightens'. Sweet, good night.	120
	This bud of love, by summer's ripening breath,
	May prove a beauteous flower when next we meet.
	Good night, good night! as sweet repose and rest
	Come to thy heart as that within my breast.

ROMEO	O wilt thou leave me so unsatisfied?	125

JULIET	What satisfaction canst thou have tonight?

ROMEO	Th'exchange of thy love's faithful vow for mine.

JULIET	I gave thee mine before thou didst request it,
	And yet I would it were to give again.

ROMEO	Wouldst thou withdraw it? For what purpose, love?	130

JULIET	But to be frank and give it thee again,
	And yet I wish but for the thing I have.
	My bounty is as boundless as the sea,
	My love as deep; the more I give to thee
	The more I have, for both are infinite.	135

The NURSE calls to JULIET from inside the house.

END OF TEST

Key Stage 3

English Test

Shakespeare Paper
The Tempest
Set B

Read this page, but don't open the booklet until your teacher says you can start. Write your name and school in the spaces below.

First Name _____

Last Name _____

School _____

Instructions

- This test is **45 minutes** long.

- You will be tested on your reading and understanding of *The Tempest*. There are **18 marks** for this paper.

- Check through all of your work carefully before the end of the test.

- If you're not sure what to do, ask your teacher.

The Tempest

Act 1 Scene 2, lines 421 to 479
Act 3 Scene 1, lines 1 to 59

In the first extract, Miranda falls in love with Ferdinand and
begs her father to be kind to him; in the second Miranda begs
Ferdinand to stop working and offers to help.

**What do you learn about Miranda's character from her
language and actions in these extracts?**

*Support your ideas by referring to both of the extracts which
are printed on the following pages.*

(18 marks)

The Tempest
Act 1 Scene 2, lines 421 to 479

> In this extract, Miranda meets Ferdinand for the first time and the couple begin to fall in love. She tries to protect Ferdinand from her father who wants to test him.

MIRANDA   I might call him
A thing divine, for nothing natural
I ever saw so noble.

PROSPERO (*Aside*)   It goes on, I see,
As my soul prompts it. (*To* ARIEL) Spirit, fine spirit!
                                                I'll free thee
Within two days for this.

FERDINAND   (*Seeing* MIRANDA) Most sure, the goddess   425
On whom these airs attend! Vouchsafe my pray'r
May know if you remain upon this island,
And that you will some good instruction give
How I may bear me here. My prime request,
Which I do last pronounce, is — O you wonder! —   430
If you be maid or no?

MIRANDA   No wonder, sir —
But certainly a maid.

FERDINAND   My language? Heavens!
I am the best of them that speak this speech,
Were I but where 'tis spoken.

PROSPERO   How the best?
What wert thou, if the King of Naples heard thee?   435

FERDINAND   A single thing, as I am now, that wonders
To hear thee speak of Naples. He does hear me,
And that he does I weep. Myself am Naples,
Who with mine eyes, never since at ebb, beheld
The King my father wrecked.

MIRANDA   Alack, for mercy!   440

FERDINAND   Yes, faith, and all his lords, the Duke of Milan
And his brave son being twain.

PROSPERO (*Aside*)   The Duke of Milan
And his more braver daughter could control thee,
If now 'twere fit to do't. At the first sight
They have changed eyes. Delicate Ariel,   445
I'll set thee free for this. (*To* FERDINAND) A word, good sir —
I fear you have done yourself some wrong — a word.

MIRANDA (*Aside*)   Why speaks my father so ungently? This
Is the third man that e'er I saw, the first

	That e'er I sighed for. Pity move my father	450
	To be inclined my way!	

FERDINAND	O, if a virgin,	
	And your affection not gone forth, I'll make you	
	The Queen of Naples.	

PROSPERO	Soft, sir, one word more!	
	(*Aside*) They are both in either's pow'rs, but this swift business	
	I must uneasy make, lest too light winning	455
	Make the prize light. (*To* FERDINAND) One word more —	
	I charge thee	
	That thou attend me — thou dost here usurp	
	The name thou ow'st not and hast put thyself	
	Upon this island as a spy, to win it	
	From me, the lord on't.	

FERDINAND	No, as I am a man.	460

MIRANDA	There's nothing ill can dwell in such a temple.	
	If the ill spirit have so fair a house,	
	Good things will strive to dwell with't.	

PROSPERO	(*To* FERDINAND) Follow me.	
	(*To* MIRANDA) Speak not you for him — he's a traitor.	
	(*To* FERDINAND) Come!	
	I'll manacle thy neck and feet together.	465
	Sea-water shalt thou drink, thy food shall be	
	The fresh-brook mussels, withered roots, and husks	
	Wherein the acorn cradled. Follow.	

FERDINAND	No —	
	I will resist such entertainment till	
	Mine enemy has more power.	

He draws his sword, and is charmed from moving.

MIRANDA	O dear father!	470
	Make not too rash a trial of him, for	
	He's gentle, and not fearful.	

PROSPERO	What, I say,	
	My foot my tutor? *(To* FERDINAND*)* Put thy sword up, traitor,	
	Who mak'st a show but dar'st not strike, thy conscience	
	Is so possessed with guilt. Come from thy ward,	475
	For I can here disarm thee with this stick	
	And make thy weapon drop.	

MIRANDA	Beseech you, father!	

PROSPERO	Hence! Hang not on my garments.	

MIRANDA	Sir, have pity.	
	I'll be his surety.	

In this extract, in order to prove his love for Miranda, Ferdinand works hard to complete the task Prospero has set him. Miranda begs Ferdinand to stop work and offers to help him.

In front of PROSPERO*'s cave.*

Enter FERDINAND, *bearing a log*

FERDINAND   There be some sports are painful, and their labour
Delight in them sets off, some kinds of baseness
Are nobly undergone, and most poor matters
Point to rich ends. This my mean task
Would be as heavy to me as odious, but   5
The mistress which I serve quickens what's dead,
And makes my labours pleasures. O, she is
Ten times more gentle than her father's crabbed,
And he's composed of harshness. I must remove
Some thousands of these logs, and pile them up,   10
Upon a sore injunction. My sweet mistress
Weeps when she sees me work, and says such baseness
Had never like executor. I forget —
But these sweet thoughts do even refresh my labours
Most busiest when I do it.

Enter MIRANDA, *and* PROSPERO *at a distance, unseen*

MIRANDA   Alas, now, pray you,   15
Work not so hard. I would the lightning had
Burnt up those logs that you are enjoined to pile.
Pray, set it down and rest you. When this burns,
'Twill weep for having wearied you. My father
Is hard at study. Pray, now, rest yourself.   20
He's safe for these three hours.

FERDINAND   O most dear mistress,
The sun will set before I shall discharge
What I must strive to do.

MIRANDA   If you'll sit down,
I'll bear your logs the while. Pray give me that,
I'll carry it to the pile.

FERDINAND   No, precious creature —   25
I had rather crack my sinews, break my back,

Than you should such dishonour undergo,
While I sit lazy by.

MIRANDA   It would become me
As well as it does you, and I should do it
With much more ease, for my good will is to it,   30
And yours it is against.

PROSPERO (*Aside*)   Poor worm, thou art infected!
This visitation shows it.

MIRANDA   You look wearily.

FERDINAND
No, noble mistress — 'tis fresh morning with me
When you are by at night. I do beseech you,
Chiefly that I might set it in my prayers,   35
What is your name?

MIRANDA   Miranda — O my father,
I have broke your hest to say so!

FERDINAND   Admired Miranda!
Indeed the top of admiration, worth
What's dearest to the world! Full many a lady
I have eyed with best regard, and many a time   40
Th' harmony of their tongues hath into bondage
Brought my too diligent ear. For several virtues
Have I liked several women, never any
With so full soul, but some defect in her
Did quarrel with the noblest grace she owed,   45
And put it to the foil — but you, O you,
So perfect and so peerless, are created
Of every creature's best!

MIRANDA   I do not know
One of my sex, no woman's face remember,
Save, from my glass, mine own, nor have I seen   50
More that I may call men than you, good friend,
And my dear father. How features are abroad,
I am skilless of, but, by my modesty,
The jewel in my dower, I would not wish
Any companion in the world but you,   55
Nor can imagination form a shape,
Besides yourself, to like of. But I prattle
Something too wildly, and my father's precepts
I therein do forget.

END OF TEST

Key Stage 3

English Test

Reading Paper
The Great Outdoors
Set C

Set C

The Great Outdoors

Read this page, but don't open the booklet until your teacher says you can start. Write your name and school in the spaces below.

First Name _____

Last Name _____

School _____

Instructions

- Before you start to write, you have **15 minutes** to read the Reading Booklet.

- From that point you will have **1 hour** to write your answers.

- Try to answer **all** of the questions.

- There are **14** questions, worth **32 marks**.

- Check through all of your work carefully before the end of the test.

- If you're not sure what to do, ask your teacher.

Questions 1-4 are about *The Bush*
(page 19 in the Reading Booklet)

1. Write down a phrase from the first three verses describing the freedom and solitude the poet finds in the bush.

....

1 mark

2. Write down two similes from the last verse.

....

....

2 marks

3. The writer repeats a phrase in the first three verses.

a) Write down the repeated phrase.

....

1 mark

b) What effect do you think the repetition of this phrase has on the reader?

....

....

1 mark

4. In the whole poem, how does the writer create a picture of the bush?

You should write about:
- descriptions of landscape;
- descriptions of plants and trees;
- the poet's attitude to the bush.

....

....

....

....

....

....

....

....

....

....

....

....

....

....

5 marks

5.   Write down one phrase from lines 1-5 that tells us that this is an important day for the narrator.

....

1 mark

6.   Write down two phrases from lines 39-49 describing the scenery.

....

....

1 mark

7.   Describe three ways in which the writer builds the feelings of tension between lines 50 and 58.

Support your answer with quotations.

....

....

....

....

....

....

....

....

3 marks

8. From lines 6-13 and 60-67, pick out four pieces of information about the techniques involved in climbing and looking after climbing equipment.

1	
2	
3	
4	

2 marks

9. Using the whole extract, explain how the writer helps the reader to understand her feelings as she sets out on the climb.

You should comment on:
- how the writer mixes information and description;
- how her language brings the scene to life;
- how successful you think she is at making the reader feel involved in the description of her experiences.

....

....

....

....

....

....

....

....

....

....

....

....

....

....

5 marks

10. From paragraph 1, pick out two words or phrases that show this magazine is written in a style designed to appeal to young people.

....

1 mark

11. From Andrew's answers in the interview, choose two statements that show he is committed to his sport. Explain your choices.

....

....

....

....

2 marks

12. From paragraphs 2 to 9 (the interview), find two quotations that suggest what Andrew is like as a person and explain what they tell you.

Quotation	What it tells you about Andrew's personality
1.	
2.	

2 marks

13. Using paragraph 9, explain why Andrew's parents decided to buy him a mountain bike.

....

1 mark

14. This question is about *Going Up* **and** *Mountain Bike Champion.*
It asks you to compare the two texts.

Write down one similarity between *Going Up* and *Mountain Bike Champion:*

....

Describe how this feature of the texts affects the reader:

....

....

Write down one difference between *Going Up* and *Mountain Bike Champion*:

....

Describe how this difference between the texts affects the reader:

....

....

4 marks

Key Stage 3

English Test

Writing Paper

Set C

Read this page, but don't open the booklet until your teacher says you can start. Write your name and school in the spaces below.

First Name _____

Last Name _____

School _____

Instructions

☐ This paper is **1 hour and 15 minutes** long.

☐ You should spend about:

45 minutes on Section A

30 minutes on Section B

☐ Section A, the longer writing task, is worth **30 marks**.

☐ Section B, the shorter writing task, is worth **20 marks**.

☐ You should spend 15 minutes planning your answer to Section A, using the planning grid provided.

☐ Check through all of your work carefully before the end of the test.

☐ If you're not sure what to do, ask your teacher.

Section A — Longer writing task

Bad Behaviour

Spend about 45 minutes on this section.

You are a pupil on the school council.

You receive this note from the head teacher:

I have been sent a letter by an elderly lady who lives near the school. She has complained about the behaviour of pupils leaving school each afternoon. She says they talk too loudly, kick footballs around and eat too many sweets.

I have already replied to her letter to explain that the pupils here are well behaved, but I think it would help if she received a letter from you as well. Please would you try to persuade her to come into school and see for herself that you and your friends are a well mannered and well behaved bunch?

You could also tell her about some of the things you and your friends do to contribute to the local community.

Write a letter to the elderly lady, persuading her that pupils at your school are well behaved and inviting her to visit so that she can see this for herself.

(30 marks)

Use this page to plan your work.

This page will not be marked.

> · Why do you think pupils at your school are well behaved?

> · What examples could you give of good behaviour?

> · How do pupils at your school make a positive contribution to the local community?

> · Why should the elderly lady visit your school?

Section B — Shorter writing task

Relaxation Area

Spend about 30 minutes on this section.

Your after-school youth club has received money to create a relaxation area and is running a competition to decide what it will be like.
The poster advertising the competition says:

Have you got a winning idea?

You're about to get a new relaxation area, but we need ideas for what it should be like.

Tell us what you think we should put in this area and why. The best idea will become reality.

Write an entry for the competition, describing the new relaxation area you would like to see and why.

(20 marks including 4 for spelling)

Key Stage 3

English Test

Shakespeare Paper
Romeo and Juliet
Set C

English

KEY STAGE
3

PRACTICE PAPER
Shakespeare
Set C

Read this page, but don't open the booklet until your teacher says you can start. Write your name and school in the spaces below.

First Name _____

Last Name _____

School _____

Instructions

- This test is **45 minutes** long.

- You will be tested on your reading and understanding of *Romeo and Juliet*. There are **18 marks** for this paper.

- Check through all of your work carefully before the end of the test.

- If you're not sure what to do, ask your teacher.

Romeo and Juliet
Act 1 Scene 1, lines 179 to 232
Act 2 Scene 2, lines 107 to 157

Imagine you are going to direct these extracts for a classroom performance.

In the first extract, Romeo tells Benvolio about Rosaline, a girl he loves.
In the second, Romeo and Juliet agree to get married.

How should the actor playing Romeo show his changing feelings about love in these extracts?

Support your ideas by referring to both of the extracts which are printed on the following pages.

(18 marks)

Romeo and Juliet
Act 1 Scene 1, lines 179 to 232

In this extract, Romeo talks to Benvolio about his feelings for Rosaline, a girl he is in love with.

ROMEO	Why, such is love's transgression.	
	Griefs of mine own lie heavy in my breast,	180
	Which thou wilt propagate, to have it pressed	
	With more of thine; this love that thou hast shown	
	Doth add more grief to too much of mine own.	
	Love is a smoke made with the fume of sighs,	
	Being purged, a fire sparkling in lovers' eyes,	185
	Being vexed a sea nourished with lovers' tears:	
	What is it else? A madness most discreet,	
	A choking gall and a preserving sweet.	
	Farewell, my coz.	
BENVOLIO	Soft! I will go along;	
	And if you leave me so, you do me wrong.	190
ROMEO	Tut, I have lost myself; I am not here,	
	This is not Romeo, he's some other where.	
BENVOLIO	Tell me in sadness, who is that you love.	
ROMEO	What, shall I groan and tell thee?	
BENVOLIO	Groan! Why no, —	
	But sadly tell me, who?	195
ROMEO	Bid a sick man in sadness make his will?	
	Ah, word ill urged to one that is so ill.	
	In sadness, cousin, I do love a woman.	
BENVOLIO	I aimed so near, when I supposed you loved.	
ROMEO	A right good mark-man! And she's fair I love.	200
BENVOLIO	A right fair mark, fair coz, is soonest hit.	
ROMEO	Well, in that hit you miss: she'll not be hit	
	With Cupid's arrow, she hath Dian's wit;	
	And, in strong proof of chastity well armed,	
	From love's weak childish bow she lives uncharmed.	205
	She will not stay the siege of loving terms,	
	Nor bide th'encounter of assailing eyes,	
	Nor ope her lap to saint-seducing gold:	

	O, she is rich in beauty, only poor,	
	That when she dies with beauty dies her store.	210
BENVOLIO	Then she hath sworn that she will still live chaste?	
ROMEO	She hath, and in that sparing makes huge waste,	
	For beauty starved with her severity	
	Cuts beauty off from all posterity.	
	She is too fair, too wise, wisely too fair,	215
	To merit bliss by making me despair:	
	She hath forsworn to love, and in that vow	
	Do I live dead that live to tell it now.	
BENVOLIO	Be ruled by me, forget to think of her.	
ROMEO	O, teach me how I should forget to think.	220
BENVOLIO	By giving liberty unto thine eyes;	
	Examine other beauties.	
ROMEO	'Tis the way	
	To call hers, exquisite, in question more:	
	These happy masks that kiss fair ladies' brows,	
	Being black puts in mind they hide the fair;	225
	He that is strucken blind cannot forget	
	The precious treasure of his eyesight lost:	
	Show me a mistress that is passing fair,	
	What doth her beauty serve, but as a note	
	Where I may read who passed that passing fair?	230
	Farewell: thou canst not teach me to forget.	
BENVOLIO	I'll pay that doctrine, or else die in debt.	

Exeunt.

> In this extract, Romeo is talking to Juliet at her balcony. They decide to get married the next day if they still feel so strongly about each other.

| ROMEO | Lady, by yonder blessèd moon I vow, |
| | That tips with silver all these fruit-tree tops — |

JULIET	O swear not by the moon, th'inconstant moon,
	That monthly changes in her circled orb,	110
	Lest that thy love prove likewise variable.

| ROMEO | What shall I swear by? |

JULIET	Do not swear at all.
	Or if thou wilt, swear by thy gracious self,
	Which is the god of my idolatry,
	And I'll believe thee.

| ROMEO | If my heart's dear love — | 115 |

JULIET	Well, do not swear. Although I joy in thee,
	I have no joy of this contract tonight,
	It is too rash, too unadvised, too sudden,
	Too like the lightning, which doth cease to be
	Ere one can say 'It lightens'. Sweet, good night.	120
	This bud of love, by summer's ripening breath,
	May prove a beauteous flower when next we meet.
	Good night, good night! as sweet repose and rest
	Come to thy heart as that within my breast.

| ROMEO | O wilt thou leave me so unsatisfied? | 125 |

| JULIET | What satisfaction canst thou have tonight? |

| ROMEO | Th'exchange of thy love's faithful vow for mine. |

| JULIET | I gave thee mine before thou didst request it, |
| | And yet I would it were to give again. |

| ROMEO | Wouldst thou withdraw it? For what purpose, love? | 130 |

JULIET	But to be frank and give it thee again,
	And yet I wish but for the thing I have.
	My bounty is as boundless as the sea,
	My love as deep; the more I give to thee
	The more I have, for both are infinite.	135

The NURSE is heard calling from inside.

ROMEO
I hear some noise within. Dear love, adieu! —
Anon, good Nurse! Sweet Montague, be true.
Stay but a little, I will come again.

Exit JULIET above

ROMEO
O blessèd, blessèd night! I am afeard,
Being in night, all this is but a dream,   140
Too flattering-sweet to be substantial.

Enter JULIET above

JULIET
Three words, dear Romeo, and good night indeed.
If that thy bent of love be honourable,
Thy purpose marriage, send me word tomorrow,
By one that I'll procure to come to thee,   145
Where and what time thou wilt perform the rite,
And all my fortunes at thy foot I'll lay,
And follow thee my lord throughout the world.

NURSE (*Calling from inside the house*)   Madam!

JULIET
I come, anon. But if thou meanest not well,   150
I do beseech thee —

NURSE (*Calling from inside the house*)   Madam!

JULIET
By and by I come —
To cease thy strife, and leave me to my grief.
Tomorrow will I send.

ROMEO
So thrive my soul —

JULIET
A thousand times good night!

Exit JULIET above

ROMEO
A thousand times the worse, to want thy light.   155
Love goes toward love as schoolboys from their books,
But love from love, toward school with heavy looks.

END OF TEST

Key Stage 3

English Test

Shakespeare Paper
The Tempest
Set C

Read this page, but don't open the booklet until your teacher says you can start. Write your name and school in the spaces below.

First Name _____

Last Name _____

School _____

Instructions

- This test is **45 minutes** long.

- You will be tested on your reading and understanding of *The Tempest*. There are **18 marks** for this paper.

- Check through all of your work carefully before the end of the test.

- If you're not sure what to do, ask your teacher.

The Tempest

Act 1 Scene 2, lines 442 to 505
Act 3 Scene 1, lines 59 to 96

In the first extract, Ferdinand and Miranda fall in love and Prospero decides to test Ferdinand. In the second, Ferdinand and Miranda promise to marry each other.

How do these extracts explore the theme of one person having power over another?

Support your ideas by referring to both of the extracts which are printed on the following pages.

(18 marks)

The Tempest
Act 1 Scene 2, lines 442 to 505

> In this extract, Miranda and Ferdinand begin to fall in love but Prospero wants to test their love for one another. He sets Ferdinand a test and makes him work for him. Miranda sticks up for Ferdinand even though Prospero tells her not to.

PROSPERO *(aside)*   The Duke of Milan
         And his more braver daughter could control thee,
         If now 'twere fit to do't. At the first sight
         They have changed eyes. Delicate Ariel,   445
         I'll set thee free for this. *(to FERDINAND)* A word, good sir —
         I fear you have done yourself some wrong — a word.

MIRANDA *(aside)*   Why speaks my father so ungently? This
         Is the third man that e'er I saw, the first
         That e'er I sighed for. Pity move my father   450
         To be inclined my way!

FERDINAND   O, if a virgin,
         And your affection not gone forth, I'll make you
         The Queen of Naples.

PROSPERO   Soft, sir, one word more!
(aside)   They are both in either's pow'rs, but this swift business
         I must uneasy make, lest too light winning   455
         Make the prize light. *(to FERDINAND)* One word more —
                             I charge thee
         That thou attend me — thou dost here usurp
         The name thou ow'st not and hast put thyself
         Upon this island as a spy, to win it
         From me, the lord on't.

FERDINAND   No, as I am a man.   460

MIRANDA   There's nothing ill can dwell in such a temple.
         If the ill spirit have so fair a house,
         Good things will strive to dwell with't.

PROSPERO   *(to FERDINAND)* Follow me.
         (to MIRANDA) Speak not you for him — he's a traitor.
                   (to FERDINAND) Come!
         I'll manacle thy neck and feet together.   465
         Sea-water shalt thou drink, thy food shall be
         The fresh-brook mussels, withered roots, and husks
         Wherein the acorn cradled. Follow.

FERDINAND   No —
         I will resist such entertainment till
         Mine enemy has more power.
         He draws, and is charmed from moving.

| MIRANDA | | O dear father, | 470 |

MIRANDA   O dear father,   470
Make not too rash a trial of him, for
He's gentle, and not fearful.

PROSPERO   What, I say,
My foot my tutor? Put thy sword up, traitor,
Who mak'st a show but dar'st not strike, thy conscience
Is so possessed with guilt. Come from thy ward,   475
For I can here disarm thee with this stick
And make thy weapon drop.

MIRANDA   Beseech you, father!

PROSPERO   Hence! Hang not on my garments.

MIRANDA   Sir, have pity.
I'll be his surety.

PROSPERO   Silence! One word more
Shall make me chide thee, if not hate thee. What!   480
An advocate for an impostor! Hush!
Thou think'st there is no more such shapes as he,
Having seen but him and Caliban. Foolish wench!
To th' most of men this is a Caliban,
And they to him are angels.

MIRANDA   My affections   485
Are then most humble. I have no ambition
To see a goodlier man.

PROSPERO   Come on — obey.
Thy nerves are in their infancy again,
And have no vigour in them.

FERDINAND   So they are.
My spirits, as in a dream, are all bound up.   490
My father's loss, the weakness which I feel,
The wreck of all my friends, nor this man's threats
To whom I am subdued, are but light to me,
Might I but through my prison once a day
Behold this maid. All corners else o' th' earth   495
Let liberty make use of. Space enough
Have I in such a prison.

PROSPERO (aside)   It works.
                        (to FERDINAND) Come on.
(to ARIEL) Thou hast done well, fine Ariel!
                        (to FERDINAND) Follow me.
(to ARIEL) Hark what thou else shalt do me.

MIRANDA   (to FERDINAND) Be of comfort.
My father's of a better nature, sir,   500
Than he appears by speech. This is unwonted
Which now came from him.

PROSPERO *(to* ARIEL*)*   Thou shalt be as free
                    As mountain winds — but then exactly do
                    All points of my command.
ARIEL   To th' syllable.
PROSPERO *(to* FERDINAND*)* Come, follow. *(to* MIRANDA*)*
                                Speak not for him.   505
                            Exeunt.

Act 3 Scene 1, lines 59 to 96

In this extract, Ferdinand follows Prospero's orders and works hard
to prove his love for Miranda. Ferdinand and Miranda talk about their feelings for
one another and agree to get married. Prospero begins to see that their love is real.

FERDINAND   I am, in my condition,
                    A prince, Miranda. I do think, a king —   60
                    I would not so — and would no more endure
                    This wooden slavery than to suffer
                    The flesh-fly blow my mouth! Hear my soul speak:
                    The very instant that I saw you, did
                    My heart fly to your service, there resides   65
                    To make me slave to it, and for your sake
                    Am I this patient log-man.

MIRANDA   Do you love me?

FERDINAND   O heaven, O earth, bear witness to this sound,
                    And crown what I profess with kind event,
                    If I speak true! If hollowly, invert   70
                    What best is boded me to mischief! I,
                    Beyond all limit of what else i' th' world,
                    Do love, prize, honour you.

MIRANDA   I am a fool
                    To weep at what I am glad of.

PROSPERO *(Aside)*   Fair encounter
                    Of two most rare affections! Heavens rain grace   75
                    On that which breeds between 'em!

FERDINAND   Wherefore weep you?

MIRANDA   At mine unworthiness, that dare not offer

	What I desire to give, and much less take	
	What I shall die to want. But this is trifling,	
	And all the more it seeks to hide itself,	80
	The bigger bulk it shows. Hence, bashful cunning,	
	And prompt me, plain and holy innocence!	
	I am your wife, if you will marry me,	
	If not, I'll die your maid. To be your fellow	
	You may deny me, but I'll be your servant,	85
	Whether you will or no.	

FERDINAND   *(He kneels)*   My mistress, dearest,
And I thus humble ever.

MIRANDA   My husband, then?

FERDINAND   Ay, with a heart as willing
As bondage e'er of freedom. Here's my hand.

MIRANDA   And mine, with my heart in't. And now farewell   90
Till half an hour hence.

FERDINAND   A thousand thousand!

Exeunt FERDINAND *and* MIRANDA *separately*

PROSPERO   So glad of this as they I cannot be,
Who are surprised withal, but my rejoicing
At nothing can be more. I'll to my book,
For yet ere supper time must I perform   95
Much business appertaining.

Exit.

END OF TEST

Answers

KS3 Maths Paper 1A Calculator NOT Allowed

Q	Marks	Correct answer	The bit in the middle tells you how to get to the answer	Useful tips

1. a | 1 | **53°** | Angles A and C are the same.

b | 2 | **127°** | Angles B and D are the same, so B = (360 − 53 − 53) ÷ 2 = 254 ÷ 2 = 127°.
(2 marks for correct answer, otherwise 1 mark for some correct working.)

2. a | 1 | **700, 0.7** | 1 cm³ = 1 ml, so 700 cm³ = 700 ml. 1000 ml = 1 litre, so 700 ml ÷ 1000 = 0.7 litres.

b | 1 | **63, 0.063** | 1000 g = 1 kg, so 63000 g ÷ 1000 = 63 kg. 1000 kg = 1 tonne, so 63 kg ÷ 1000 = 0.063 tonnes.

3. | 2 | | **(2 marks for correct answer, otherwise 1 mark for correct enlargement but wrong position.)** | *TIP: A scale factor of ½ means the lines on your new shape should be <u>half as long</u>, and each point should be <u>half the distance</u> from the centre.*

4. | 2 |

	Theme Park	Seaside	Total
Boys	41	**23**	**64**
Girls	**42**	14	56
Total	**83**	**37**	120

(2 marks for correctly completed table, otherwise 1 mark for at least three correct values.)

5. a | 1 | **Both Julia and Gazza are correct.** | The expressions are the same. Two lengths of n and two of 10.

b | 2 | **$4n + 10$** | $2n + 2n + 5 + 5 = 4n + 10$. One mark for this working.

c | 2 | **$n + 40$** | $\frac{n}{2} + \frac{n}{2} + 4 \times 10 = n + 40$. One mark for a correct expression and one for simplifying.

d | 1 | **$n = 10$** | The perimeters are equal when $n + 40 = 4n +10$. $3n = 30$. **$n = 10$**

TIPS: Don't worry about n, it just stands for any number.

6. | 4 |

```
    6              21             25
3  54  18      7  84  12     12.5  5³  10
    9               4              5
```

(4 marks for all six correct values, otherwise 3 marks for five correct, 2 marks for four correct or 1 mark for two or three correct.)

7. | 2 | **64 minutes** | £8.96 = 896p, 896 ÷ 14 = 64 minutes.
(2 marks for correct answer, otherwise 1 mark for some correct working.)

8. a | 1 | **x = -6** | $\frac{3x}{9} = -2$, 3x = -18, x = -6

b | 1 | **y = 15** | 2y − 6 = 24, 2y = 30, y = 15

c | 2 | **z = 18** | 3z − 7 = 29 + z, 3z − z = 29 + 7, 2z = 36, z = 18
(2 marks for correct answer, otherwise 1 mark for some correct working.)

TIP: Always <u>check</u> your answers by putting them back into the equations.

9. a | 1 | **25%** | $\frac{90}{360} \times 100 = 25\%$

b | 2 | **216°** | $\frac{60}{100} \times 360 = 216°$ *TIP: Remember — with pie charts, 360° always represents 100% of the data.*
(2 marks for correct answer, otherwise 1 mark for some correct working.)

| c | 2 | **2000** | $100 - 25 - 60 = 15\%$ of people are not registered with a dentist. $15\% = 300$ people. So $1\% = 300 \div 15 = 20$. $100\% = 20 \times 100 = 2000$ people. **(2 marks for correct answer, otherwise 1 mark for some correct working.)** |

| 10. a | 1 | $\dfrac{1}{4}$ | $\dfrac{3}{4} - \dfrac{1}{2} = \dfrac{1}{4}$ |
| b | 2 | $\dfrac{5}{8}$ | $\dfrac{3}{4} + \dfrac{5}{8} + \dfrac{1}{2} = \dfrac{6}{8} + \dfrac{5}{8} + \dfrac{4}{8} = \dfrac{15}{8}$. $\dfrac{15}{8} \div 3 = \dfrac{5}{8}$ **(2 marks for correct answer, otherwise 1 mark for finding the sum of the fractions.)** |

TIP: To add fractions you need to put them over a common denominator.

| 11. | 3 | **24 teachers and 84 pupils** | $2 + 7 = 9$, so 1 part $= 108 \div 9 = 12$. $12 \times 2 = 24$ teachers, $12 \times 7 = 84$ pupils. **(3 marks for correct answer, otherwise 1 mark for some correct working and 1 mark for either 24 or 84.)** |

| 12. a | 2 | **x = 12** | $4x + 30 = 78$, $4x = 78 - 30$, $4x = 48$, $x = 12$ **(1 mark for correct algebraic expression and 1 mark for correct answer.)** |
| b | 1 | **2008** | $2020 - 12 = 2008$ |

13. a	1	**-47**	$y = (-2 \times 25) + 3 = -47$
b	1	**17**	$-31 = -2x + 3$, $2x = 34$, $x = 17$
c	3	**(2.5, -2)**	$-2x + 3 = 6x - 17$, $3 + 17 = 6x + 2x$, $20 = 8x$, $x = 2.5$. So $y = -2x + 3 = (-2 \times 2.5) + 3 = -5 + 3 = -2$. **(3 marks for a correct method and correct answer, otherwise 2 marks for a correct method and either x or y correct, or 1 mark for some correct working.)**

TIP: You can also solve part (c) by using a simultaneous equations method.

14. a	1	**0.68**	$0.42 + 0.26 = 0.68$
b	1	**0.32**	$1 - (0.42 + 0.26) = 1 - 0.68 = 0.32$
c	1	**21**	Number of peanuts $= 0.42 \times 50 = 21$

TIP: All the probabilities must add up to 1.

| 15. | 3 | **15%** | $0.75 \times 0.2 = 0.15$, $0.15 \times 100 = 15\%$ **(3 marks for correct answer, otherwise 1-2 marks for some correct working.)** |

| 16. a | 1 | $d = \dfrac{e - 6}{2}$ | $2d + 6 = e$, $2d = e - 6$, $d = \dfrac{e - 6}{2}$ |
| b | 2 | $f = \sqrt{\dfrac{3g - 8}{5}}$ | $8 + 5f^2 = 3g$, $5f^2 = 3g - 8$, $f^2 = \dfrac{3g - 8}{5}$, $f = \sqrt{\dfrac{3g - 8}{5}}$ **(2 marks for correct answer, otherwise 1 mark for some correct working.)** |

17. a	2	$0.03 \times 0.1 = 0.003$	**(One mark for selecting the correct numbers)**
b	1	$20 \div 0.1 = 200$	Dividing by 0.1 is the same as multiplying by 10.
c	1	$\dfrac{2}{p}$	Dividing by a number between 0 and 1 is the same as multiplying by a number. So the result will be > 2 and therefore bigger than all the others.

| 18. a | 2 | **36 cm** | Ratio of kites $= 25 : 10 = 5 : 2$. 1 part $= 90 \div 5 = 18$ cm. $2 \times 18 = 36$ cm. **(2 marks for correct answer, otherwise 1 mark for some correct working.)** |
| b | 1 | **120°** | Similar shapes have the same angles. |

KS3 Maths Paper 1B Calculator Allowed

Q	Marks	Correct answer	The bit in the middle tells you how to get to the answer	Useful tips

1. a | 1 | **1.175768662**

b | 1 | **1.176**

c | 1 | **3.2**

TIP: Remember — you need to use <u>BODMAS</u> to tell the calculator which <u>order</u> to do things in.

---

2. a | 1 | **Eight out of the twenty squares should be shaded.** $\dfrac{4}{10} = \dfrac{8}{20}$

b | 1 | **0.55**   22 out of 40 = 22 ÷ 40 = 0.55

c | 1 | **62.5%**   40 out of 64, so (40 ÷ 64) × 100 = 62.5%

---

3. a | 2 | **(2 marks for correct answer, otherwise 1 mark for at least 2 squares shaded correctly.)**

b | 2 | or 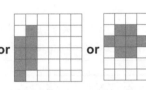 or ... or ...

TIP: When you've finished your pattern <u>turn the page round</u> through 360° and check that there are only two positions where it looks the same.

(2 marks for correct answer, otherwise 1 mark for at least 2 squares shaded correctly.)

---

4. a | 1 | $\dfrac{21}{40}$ There are 15 + 2 + 4 = 21 boys out of a total of 15 + 2 + 4 + 3 + 11 + 5 = 40 students.

b | 1 | $\dfrac{9}{40}$ 4 boys + 5 girls = 9 students play the keyboard out of a total of 40 students.

c | 1 | $\dfrac{3}{18}$ or $\dfrac{1}{6}$ There are 3 girl guitarists out of a total of 15 boys + 3 girls = 18 students who play guitar.

---

5. a | 1 | **£2.88**   36p × 8 = 288p = £2.88

b | 2 | **Shop A by 9p**   At shop A it costs 36p × 18 = £6.48, at shop B it costs £2.19 × 3 = £6.57. £6.57 – £6.48 = 9p

(2 marks for correct working and answer, otherwise 1 mark for getting both £6.48 and £6.57.)

---

6. | 2 | **20 weeks** 105 – 77 = 28, 28 ÷ 1.4 = 20 weeks.

(2 marks for correct answer, otherwise 1 mark for some correct working.)

---

7. a | 1 | **2s + 4**

b | 1 | **11t² + 3t**

c | 1 | **18u²**

d | 1 | **4v²**

---

8. a | 2 |

Speed (s) in mph	frequency (f)	midpoint (x)	fx
90 < s ≤ 100	12	95	1140
100 < s ≤ 110	18	105	1890
110 < s ≤ 120	28	115	3220
120 < s ≤ 130	7	125	875
Total	65	-	7125

(2 marks for all six correct values, otherwise 1 mark for at least three.)

b | 1 | **109.6 mph**   7125 ÷ 65 = 109.6 mph (to 1 d.p.)

9.	4	**a = 50°, b = 40°, c = 200°, d = 70°**

a = 360° – 130° – 90° – 90° = 50°. b = 130° – 90° = 40°.
c = 360° – 160° = 200°. d = 180° – 110° = 70°.

TIP: These questions shouldn't cause any bother if you've learnt the angle rules.

(1 mark for each correct angle.)

---

10. a	2	**£350** £287 is 100% – 18% = 82% of the original price. 1% = 287 ÷ 82 = 3.5, so 100% = 3.5 × 100 = £350.

(2 marks for correct answer, otherwise 1 mark for some correct working.)

b	2	**55%** 120 – 54 = 66 photos are discarded, $\frac{66}{120} \times 100 = 55\%$.

(2 marks for correct answer, otherwise 1 mark for some correct working.)

11.	2	**339.3 cm³** Volume = $\pi r^2 h = \pi \times 3^2 \times 12 = 339.3$ cm³ (to 1 d.p.)

(2 marks for correct answer, otherwise 1 mark for substituting correctly into the formula.)

12.	2	**5.7 seconds** Time = distance/speed, so the times are 40 ÷ 12.5 = 3.2 and 40 ÷ 16 = 2.5. 3.2 + 2.5 = 5.7 s.

(2 marks for correct answer, otherwise 1 mark for either 3.2 or 2.5.)

13.	3	**24 newspapers**

Let x = number of newspapers delivered on Tuesday. So 3.5x + 30 = 114, 3.5x = 114 – 30 = 84, x = 24.

(3 marks for correct answer, otherwise 1 mark for correct equation and 1 mark for attempting to solve it.)

14.	2	**x² + 3x – 28** (x + 7)(x – 4) = x² – 4x + 7x – 28 = x² + 3x – 28.

(2 marks for correct answer, otherwise 1 mark for getting 2 out of 3 terms correct.)

---

15. a	1	**P is (0 , 1). Q is (1 , 3)**
b	2	**2** Gradient of line = change in y ÷ change in x = (3 – 1) ÷ (1 – 0) = 2 ÷ 1 = 2.

(2 marks for correct answer, or 1 mark for using the correct method but getting the wrong answer.)

c	1	**y = 2x + 1** The gradient is 2 and it crosses the y-axis at 1, so the equation must be y = 2x + 1.

---

16. a	2	**Body mass index = 22.9 (3 s.f.) or 22.86 (4 s.f.), Weight status = Normal**

Body mass index = 70 ÷ 1.75² = 22.857...

(1 mark for correct body mass index, 1 mark for correct weight status.)

b	2	**1.70 m** h² = 55 ÷ 19 = 2.8947..., h = $\sqrt{2.8947...}$ = 1.70 m (2 d.p.)

(2 marks for correct answer, otherwise 1 mark for some correct working.)

c	3	**11 kg** For body mass index of 28, weight = 28 × 1.64² = 75.3088 kg.

For body mass index of 24, weight = 24 × 1.64² = 64.5504 kg.
Weight loss = 75.3088 – 64.5504 = 10.7584 = 11 kg (to nearest kilogram).

(3 marks for correct answer, otherwise 1 mark for each correct weight.)

---

17. a	2	**78 m** (AB)² = 30² + 72² = 900 + 5184 = 6084, AB = $\sqrt{6084}$ = 78 m

(2 marks for correct answer, otherwise 1 mark for some correct working.)

b	2	**22.6°** $a = \tan^{-1}\left(\frac{30}{72}\right) = 22.6°$

(2 marks for correct answer, otherwise 1 mark for some correct working.)

---

18. a	1	**0.4** 1 – 0.6 = 0.4
b	1	**12 days** 0.4 × 30 = 12
c	1	**0.216** 0.6 × 0.6 × 0.6 = 0.216

TIP: To work out the expected number of days you just multiply the probability for one day by the total number of days. Easy.

KS3 Maths Paper 2A Calculator NOT Allowed

Q	Marks	Correct answer	The bit in the middle tells you how to get to the answer	Useful tips

1. a | 1 | **4/15** | There are four raspberry flavour out of a total of fifteen.

b | 1 | **9/15 or 3/5** | There are nine sweets that are not blackberry out of fifteen.

c | 1 | **Cannot tell. You don't know how many sweets are in his bag so you don't know if half of them is more or less than the 5 Debbie has.**
(Only award mark for "Cannot tell" <u>and</u> a correct explanation.)

2. a | 3 | To construct the triangle draw the base the correct length first.
Use compasses set to 5 cm and 4 cm from each end of the base to draw arcs.
Where the arcs cross gives the position for B.
(3 marks for correct answer, otherwise 2 marks for two sides the correct length, or 1 mark for one side the correct length.)

b | 1 | **40 – 43°**

3. | 2 | **£115** | Use 50 as an estimate of the number of calculators and £2.30 as an estimate of the cost.
So 2.30 × 50 = 2.30 × 10 × 5 = 23 × 5 = £115. **(2 marks for correct answer (also accept 2 × 50 = £100), otherwise 1 mark for evidence of sensible rounding.)**

4. a | 1 | **£99** | (7 × 12) + 15 = 84 + 15 = £99

b | 2 | **11 days** | Work backwards through the number machine: 147 – 15 = 132, 132 ÷ 12 = 11.
(2 marks for correct answer, otherwise 1 mark for some correct working.)

c | 1 | **The delivery charge**

5. a | 1 | **x = 6** | 3x + 7 = 25, 3x = 18, x = 18 ÷ 3 = 6
b | 1 | **x = 9.5** | 4(x − 2) = 30, 4x − 8 = 30, 4x = 38, x = 9.5
c | 1 | **x = -4** | 2x − 9 = 5x + 3, -3x = 12, x = -4

TIP: There are several different methods for solving equations. Trial and error can work well for simple ones like part (a). But for more complicated ones you really need to know how to <u>multiply out brackets</u> and <u>collect like terms</u>.

6. a | 1 | **-5**
b | 1 | **-3**
c | 1 | **4**
d | 1 | **12**

TIP: Remember the <u>rules</u> for adding and subtracting <u>negative numbers</u> — "+ +" and "– –" mean add, but "+ –" means subtract.

7. a | 1 | **144 cm³** | 6 × 6 × 4 = 144 cm³

b | 2 | **168 cm²** | Area of side faces = 6 × 4 = 24. Area of top and bottom faces = 6 × 6 = 36.
Total surface area = (4 × 24) + (2 × 36) = 96 + 72 = 168 cm².
(2 marks for correct answer, otherwise 1 mark for some correct working.)

c | 2 | OR | **(2 marks for correct answer (the cuboids can be drawn in different positions), otherwise 1 mark for a cuboid with two dimensions correct.)**

TIP: The easiest way to think about this is that the volume of a 2 cm cube is 2³ = 8 cm³. So to make a cuboid of volume 48 cm³, you need 48 ÷ 8 = 6 cubes.

8. a | 1 | **20%** | 3 + 5 + 2 = 10, (2 ÷ 10) × 100 = 20%

b | 2 | **30 geese, 12 swans** | 18 ducks are 3 parts of the bird population, so 1 part is 18 ÷ 3 = 6.
Geese = 5 × 6 = 30, swans = 2 × 6 = 12 **(1 mark for each correct answer.)**

9. a | 3 | **0.2, 0.3, ²⁄₅, ½** | Turn the fractions into decimals: 1 ÷ 2 = 0.5. 2 ÷ 5 = 0.4.
So the order is 0.2, 0.3, ²⁄₅, ½.
(1 mark for 0.2 first, 1 mark for ½ last, 1 mark for middle terms in correct order.)

10. | 2

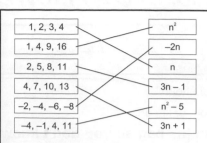

(**2 marks matching all five expressions correctly, 1 mark for matching three or four options correctly.**)

---

11. a | 1 | **50°F** $F = \dfrac{9C}{5} + 32 = \dfrac{9 \times 10}{5} + 32 = 18 + 32 = 50°F$

TIP: When you're working things out without a calculator remember to <u>simplify</u> as much as possible. (9 × -20) ÷ 5 becomes a lot easier if you cancel the 5 first. Then it's just 9 × -4 which is -36.

b | 2 | **-4°F** $F = \dfrac{9C}{5} + 32 = \dfrac{9 \times -20}{5} + 32 = -36 + 32 = -4°F$

(**2 marks for correct answer, otherwise 1 mark for substituting -20 into formula but then making one error.**)

c | 2 | **$C = \dfrac{5(F - 32)}{9}$** $F = \dfrac{9C}{5} + 32$, $F - 32 = \dfrac{9C}{5}$, $5(F - 32) = 9C$, $C = \dfrac{5(F - 32)}{9}$

(**2 marks for correct answer, otherwise 1 mark for completing the first step to get $F - 32 = \dfrac{9C}{5}$.**)

---

12. | 2 | **No. The numbers do not fit Pythagoras' Theorem. $6^2 = 36$ but $5^2 + 4^2 = 25 + 16 = 41$.**

(**2 marks for No and correct explanation, otherwise 1 mark for showing use of Pythagoras' Theorem.**)

---

13. | 2 | **$x^2 + 9x + 20$** $(x + 5)(x + 4) = x^2 + 4x + 5x + 20 = x^2 + 9x + 20$

(**2 marks for correct answer, otherwise 1 mark for an unsimplified expression with at least three terms correct.**)

TIP: You'll have no trouble with these if you've learnt the foolproof <u>FOIL</u> method.

---

14. a | 2

	1	2	3	4	5	6
1	1	2	3	4	5	6
2	2	4	6	8	10	12
3	3	6	9	12	15	18

(**2 marks for all twelve correct values, otherwise 1 mark for at least six correct values.**)

b | 1 | **6/18 or 1/3** Six out of the eighteen scores are odd.

---

15. | 3 | **x = 1.5 and y = 3**

The perimeter of the triangle is 36, so because it's an equilateral triangle, every side must be 36 ÷ 3 - 12. So 8x = 12, which gives x = 12 ÷ 8 = 1.5.
Then 2x + 3y = 12 = (2 × 1.5) + 3y = 12, or 3y = 9, giving y = 3.
(**3 marks for the correct answers. If an answer is wrong, then 1 mark for finding the length of each side ad 1 mark for each x and y.**)

---

16. a | 3

Number of cakes per box	100	**250**	500	**1000**	2000	5000
Number of boxes	**100**	40	20	10	**5**	2

100 ÷ 4 = 250.   100000 ÷ 10 = 1000
10000 ÷ 100 = 100   10000 ÷ 2000 = 5

b | 1 | **T = N × B** The batch of cakes has to be put into N boxes, each containing B cakes.

c | 2 | **3 hours 20 minutes** 10000 ÷ 50 = 200 minutes = 2 hours and 20 minutes.

---

17. a | 1 | **29030**

b | 2 | **2.462×10^4** $29030 - 4410 = 24620 = 2.462 \times 10^4$

(**2 marks for correct answer, otherwise 1 mark for correct calculation but answer not in standard form.**)

---

18. a | 1 | **y = 0** Anything to the power 0 is 1.

b | 1 | **y = 4**

c | 1 | **y = 2** $72 = y^3 \times 3^2$, $y^3 = 72 \div 9 = 8$, $\sqrt[3]{8} = 2$

TIP: Parts (b) and (c) look tricky, but don't panic — you can work them out by trial and error. Sub in values of y (1, 2, etc.) and you soon get the right answer.

KS3 Maths Paper 2B Calculator Allowed

Q	Marks	Correct answer	The bit in the middle tells you how to get to the answer	Useful tips

1. a 1

b 1

TIP: With <u>rotations</u>, use tracing paper to help find the centre of rotation.
With <u>reflections</u>, each point of the new shape should be <u>exactly the same distance</u> away from the mirror line as the corresponding point of the old shape.

---

2. 3

Number of 5p coins	Number of 10p coins	Number of 20p coins
1	0	2
1	2	1
3	1	1
5	0	1
1	4	0
2	3	0
5	2	0
7	1	0
9	0	0

(3 marks for all eight different ways, otherwise 2 marks for five to seven ways or 1 mark for at least three ways.)

---

3. a 1 E.g.

4/7 × 21 = 12 (shade any 12 squares)

b 1 E.g.

0.3 × 20 = 6 (shade any 6 squares)

c 1 E.g.

45/100 × 20 = 9 (shade any 9 squares)

TIP: Just count the number of squares and times by the proportion. Easy!

---

4. a 1 **35 minutes**   52 – 17 = 35

b 1 **31 minutes**   order list: 17 26 31 43 52, middle number = 31.

c 2 E.g. **20 23 25 30 40 (1 mark for a list with 25 as the median, 1 mark for a list with a range of 20.)**

---

5. a 2 **30**   108 ÷ 9 = 12° per student. 360° ÷ 12 = 30
(2 marks for correct answer, otherwise 1 mark for some correct working.)

b 1 **Cannot tell**
A bigger proportion of 9A have dogs, but you don't know how many students are in 9B.
(Only award the mark for "Cannot tell" and a correct explanation.)

---

6. a 2 E.g. **(0, 7), (1, 6), (2, 5)**
(2 marks for three pairs that fit the rule, otherwise 1 mark for two pairs that fit the rule.)

b 2

TIP: In part (a) you handily found three points on the line x + y = 7. So just plot them and join with a straight line.

(1 mark for plotting at least three correct points and 1 mark for joining them with a straight line.)

---

7. 2

Keeping your compass setting the same, draw two arcs from each cross.
Draw a straight line between the two points where the arcs cross. This is the perpendicular bisector.
(2 marks for correct answer, otherwise 1 mark for drawing arcs (or circles) to give at least two points on the locus.)

---

8. a 2 **11.2%**   Increase in salary = £3600, (3600 ÷ 32 200) × 100 = 11.180... = 11.2% (1 d.p.).
(2 marks for correct answer, otherwise 1 mark for 3600.)

b 2 **£26 542**   28 400 = 107%, so 1% = 28 400 ÷ 107 = 265.4205..., so 100% = 100 × 265.4205... = 26 542.05...
= £26 542 (nearest £) **(2 marks for correct answer, otherwise 1 mark for some correct working.)**

Answers

9.	a	1	**28**	$4 + 9 + 8 + 5 + 2 = 28$

9. b 3 **6 hours and 40 minutes**

Multiply all frequencies by the mid values of the groups: $(4 \times 1.5) + (9 \times 4.5) + (8 \times 7.5) + (5 \times 10.5) + (2 \times 13.5) = 186$, $186 \div 28 = 6.642...$ hours. $0.642...$ hours $\times 60 = 38.57...$ mins, so 6 hours 40 mins to the nearest 10 mins.

(3 marks for correct answer. Otherwise 2 marks for correct calculations but answer not rounded, or 1 mark for getting 186.)

---

10. a 2 **10**

Circumference $= 2\pi r = 2\pi = 6.28...$ cm. $65 \div 6.28... = 10.34...$, so 10 complete revolutions.
(2 marks for correct answer, otherwise 1 mark for correctly finding circumference.)

b 2 **3.14 cm²** Area $= \pi r^2 = \pi \times 1^2 = 3.14$ cm² (3 s.f.)
(2 marks for correct answer, or 1 mark for using correct formula but with a calculation error.)

c 3 **43**

Radius of real wheel $= \sqrt{(0.58 \div \pi)} = 0.429...$ m $= 0.43$ m (2 d.p.).
Radius of toy wheel $= 1$ cm $= 0.01$ m. So scale factor $= 0.43 \div 0.01 = 43$.
(3 marks for correct answer, otherwise 1 mark for finding radius of real wheel and 1 mark for finding radius of toy wheel in same units as real wheel.)

---

11. a 1 **18°** $180° - 162° = 18°$

b 1 **20** $360° \div 18° = 20$ sides

*TIP: Remember the **rule**: exterior angle = 360° ÷ no. of sides. So just rearrange to find the number of sides.*

---

12. a 1 **30.9 mph** $\dfrac{18}{35} \times 60 = 30.9$ mph (3 s.f.)

b 1 **28.4 minutes** $\dfrac{18}{38} \times 60 = 28.4$ minutes (3 s.f.)

TIP: Watch out with these. You need to multiply or divide by 60 to change the time from minutes into hours or vice versa.

c 1 **16.7 miles** $\dfrac{25}{60} \times 40 = 16.7$ miles (3 s.f.)

---

13. a 2 **x = 8.05 cm** $x^2 = 3.4^2 + 7.3^2 = 64.85$, $\sqrt{64.85} = 8.05$ cm (3 s.f.)
(2 marks for correct answer, otherwise 1 mark for correct use of Pythagoras' theorem.)

b 2 **x = 2.68 cm** $x^2 = 6.3^2 - 5.7^2 = 7.2$, $\sqrt{7.2} = 2.68$ cm (3 s.f.)
(2 marks for correct answer, otherwise 1 mark for correct use of Pythagoras' theorem.)

---

14. a 2 **195.4 cm³** $V = \dfrac{4}{3} \times \pi \times 3.6^3 = 195.432... = 195$ cm³ (3 s.f.)

(2 marks for correct answer, otherwise 1 mark for correct substitution into formula.)

b 2 **1.89 cm** $r = \sqrt[3]{\dfrac{3V}{4\pi}} = \sqrt[3]{\dfrac{3 \times 28.3}{4\pi}} = \sqrt[3]{6.756} = 1.89$ cm (3 s.f.)

(2 marks for correct answer, otherwise 1 mark for correctly rearranging formula for r.)

---

15. a 2 **a = 21.3°** $\tan a = \dfrac{4.8}{12.3}$, $a = \tan^{-1}\left(\dfrac{4.8}{12.3}\right) = 21.317... = 21.3°$ (3 s.f.)

(2 marks for correct answer, otherwise 1 mark for use of tan.)

b 2 **b = 2.60 cm** $\sin 32° = b/4.9$, so $b = \sin 32° \times 4.9 = 2.596... = 2.60$ cm (3 s.f.)
(2 marks for correct answer, otherwise 1 mark for use of sin.)

---

16. a 2 **3a + 2c = 31, 2a + 5c = 39** **(1 mark for each equation.)**

b 2 **a = £7, c = £5** To get 6a in both equations, multiply the first by 2 and the second by 3 to get $6a + 4c = 62$ and $6a + 15c = 117$. Now subtract the first from the second to get $11c = 55$ and so $c = 5$. $3a + 2c = 31$, so $3a = 21$ and $a = 7$.
(2 marks for correct working and answer, otherwise 1 mark for some correct working and either a or c.)

---

17. a 2 **x = 4.8 cm, y = 8.75 cm** From rectangle B, ratio of length and width is $8 \div 5 = 1.6$. $x = 3 \times 1.6 = 4.8$ cm and $y = 14 \div 1.6 = 8.75$ cm. **(1 mark for each correct length.)**

b 1 **12/35 or 0.34** A is smaller than C so the scale factor is less than 1. $4.8 \div 14 = 48/140 = 12/35$ (or 0.34 (2 s.f.)).
(2 marks for correct answer, otherwise 1 mark for some correct working.)

KS3 Maths Paper 3A Calculator NOT Allowed

Q	Marks	Correct answer	The bit in the middle tells you how to get to the answer	Useful tips

1. a | 1 | $8 \times 30 = 240$, $8 \times 7 = 56$, $240 + 56 = 296$ (or do a multiplication showing that a 5 must be carried).

b | 2 | **1184** | 32×37 is 4 lots of 8×37, 4×296 is $4 \times (300 - 4) = 1200 - 16 = 1184$.
(2 marks for correct answer, otherwise 1 mark for saying that you need to find 4 lots of 296, or trying to do that multiplication sum.)

2. a | 1 | **d + 10**

b | 1 | **k − 7**

c | 1 | **3d**

d | 1 | **3d − d = 2d**

e | 2 | **2d − k** | The difference between their ages is d − k, so in d − k years time Katya will be David's age now. His age then is d + d − k, which is 2d − k.
(2 marks for correct answer, otherwise 1 mark for getting d − k.)

3. | 2 | **10 cm** | Area = ½ × base × height. So 100 = ½ × 20 × height, or 100 = 10 × height. So height = 100 ÷ 10 = 10 cm. **(One mark only for correct working but wrong answer.)**

4. a | 2 | **No — Because some multiples of 3 are even, e.g. 6.**
(1 mark for saying no, and 1 mark for the correct explanation.)

b | 2 | **"It is a multiple of 3" and "It is divisible by 6" should be ticked.**
(2 marks for correct answer, otherwise 1 mark for 1 correct and 1 wrong statement ticked.)

5. a | 1 | **11** | The number of grey crosses is one more than the pattern number.

b | 1 | **20** | The number of white crosses is double the pattern number.

c | 1 | **301** | 101 grey + 200 white = 301 crosses altogether.

6. a | 1 | $\dfrac{12}{35}$ | $\dfrac{1}{7} + \dfrac{1}{5} = \dfrac{5}{35} + \dfrac{7}{35} = \dfrac{12}{35}$

b | 1 | $\dfrac{4}{39}$ | $\dfrac{2}{13} - \dfrac{2}{39} = \dfrac{6}{39} - \dfrac{2}{39} = \dfrac{4}{39}$

TIP: Don't always just times the two denominators — you're looking for the smallest number both denominators go into.

7. a | 1 | **30%**

b | 1 | **No. The graph just shows the percentage increase in sales, not the sales themselves. So Company B would have large increases but a much smaller number of sales.**

c | 1 | **No. The percentage increase in sales was less but it was still an increase in sales.**

8. a | 1 | **Width = y cm, Length = 2x cm**

b | 2 | The scale factor of the enlargement is new length ÷ old length = 2x ÷ y, or new width ÷ old width = y ÷ x, so $\dfrac{2x}{y} = \dfrac{y}{x}$.
(2 marks for correct explanation, otherwise 1 mark for referring to scale factor of enlargement or use of ratios.)

c | 1 | $y = \sqrt{2}x$ | Sophie is incorrect because she hasn't square rooted both sides of the equation correctly.
$\dfrac{2x}{y} = \dfrac{y}{x}$, so $y^2 = 2x^2$, so $y = \sqrt{2x^2} = \sqrt{2}x$

9. a | **1** | **2 cm** | $4\pi = \pi r^2$, $r^2 = 4$ so $r = 2$ cm

b | **2** | Hypotenuse is the diameter = 4 cm. Using Pythagoras, $\left(\sqrt{8}\right)^2 + AC^2 = 4^2$, so $AC^2 = 16 - 8 = 8$, so $AC = \sqrt{8}$.
AC = BC, so the triangle is isosceles. **(1 mark for using Pythagoras and 1 mark for showing AC = $\sqrt{8}$.)**

c | **1** | **4 cm²** | ½ × base × height = ½ × $\sqrt{8}$ × $\sqrt{8}$ = 4 cm²

---

10. a | **1** | **1. modal age, 2. median age, 3. mean age**

b | **1** | **The mean is largest because it takes into account the ages of the adults, the others don't.**

TIP: You can see straight away that the modal age is 3. And the median must be either 3 or 4. A quick count up of the people gives 51 in total, so the median is 4.

---

11. a | **1** | $\dfrac{1}{8}$ | $\dfrac{3}{24} = \dfrac{1}{8}$

b | **3** | **Small** | Probability of small tin being peaches is 3/10, probability of large tin being peaches is 4/14 = 2/7.
2/7 = 20/70, 3/10 = 21/70. So probability is higher with small tin.
(1 mark for saying "small", 1 mark for 3/10 and 2/7, and 1 mark for showing 3/10 is larger.)

---

12. a | **2** | Angle PTQ is y because triangle PTQ is isosceles, so angle PQT is 180° − 2y. Angle PQT + x = 180°, so PQT = 180° − x. So 180° − 2y = 180° − x, -2y = -x, x = 2y.
(2 marks for correct explanation, otherwise 1 mark for getting angle PQT = 180° − 2y or 180° − x.)

TIP: It's often a good idea to try and work out as many angles as you can. Then see what information you can use to answer the question.

b | **2** | **y = 30°** | Angle TSQ = x as triangle TSQ is isosceles. Angle PTS = 90°.
So using triangle PTS, 180° = 90° + y + x, 180° = 90° + y + 2y, 3y = 90°, y = 30°.
(2 marks for correct answer, otherwise 1 mark for some correct working.)

TIP: Remember to use x = 2y from part (a).

---

13. a | **1** | **£20** | 200 ÷ 10 = 20

b | **1** | **£5** | 2½% is 10% ÷ 4, 20 ÷ 4 = 5

c | **2** | **£269.50** | 10% = 22, 2½% = 5.50, so 22½% = 22 + 22 + 5.5 = 49.50
Total price = 220 + 49.50 = £269.50
(2 marks for correct answer. otherwise 1 mark for finding 10% and 2½% correctly.)

---

14. a | **1** | **When x is even, x(x + 3) is even**

b | **1** | **When x is odd, x² + 1 is even**

c | **1** | **x² + x is always even.**

The simplest way to tackle questions like these is to pick an even or an odd number and substitute it into the equation.

---

15. | **2** | **2, 2, 3, 4, 9 or 2, 2, 3, 5, 8 or 2, 2, 3, 6, 7**
(2 marks for correct answer, otherwise 1 mark for 2, 2, 3 and two other numbers.)

TIP: You need to narrow down the options. The list has to begin 2, 2, 3,... and a mean of 4 means the five numbers have to sum to 20.

---

16. a | **2** | **57 cm²** | ½ × (12 + 7) × 6 = ½ × 6 × 19 = 3 × 19 = 57 cm²
(2 marks for correct answer, otherwise 1 mark for some correct working.)

b | **2** | **684 cm³** | Cross-sectional area × depth = 57 × 12 = 684 cm³.
(2 marks for correct answer, otherwise 1 mark for attempting to multiply area by depth. Award marks for correctly calculated answer using incorrect value from part (a).)

---

17. a | **1** | **Negative correlation**

b | **2** | **Intercept must be more than 20. Gradient must be negative.** **(1 mark for each correct reason.)**

---

18. a | **1** | **1547** | 2.38 × 650 = 23.8 ÷ 10 × 6.5 × 100 = 154.7 × 10 = 1547

TIP: Make sure your answers are sensible. For example, to work out "2.38 × 650", think, "two and a bit times 650 is going to be one thousand and something".

b | **1** | **0.65** | $\dfrac{154.7}{23.8} = 6.5$, so $\dfrac{154.7}{238} = \dfrac{6.5}{10} = 0.65$

c | **1** | **238** | $\dfrac{154.7}{6.5} = 23.8$, so $\dfrac{15.47}{0.065} = 23.8 \times \dfrac{100}{10} = 238$

Q	Marks	Correct answer	The bit in the middle tells you how to get to the answer	Useful tips

1. a | 1 | **2**

b | 1 | **-10**

c | 1 | **8**

TIP: _Careful_ with powers — in part (c) you only square the x, not the whole thing.

---

2. a | 2 | **BestXchange**

BetaTravel gives 82 ÷ 60 = 1.366... euros for £1, or 60 ÷ 82 = £0.731... for 1 euro.
BestXchange gives 100 ÷ 72 = 1.388... euros for £1, or 72 ÷ 100 = £0.72 for 1 euro.
So BestXchange is better value.
(1 mark for correct calculation of either rate and 1 mark for correct answer.)

b | 1 | **138.89 euros**

$\frac{100}{72} \times 100 = 138.89$ euros

---

3. a | 1 | **a = 65°**

PQR is an isosceles triangle, so a must be = 65°.

b | 1 | **b = 65°**

b is the alternate angle to a and so must be the same.

c | 1 | **c = 115°**

b + c = 180°, so c = 180° − 65° = 115°.

d | 1 | **d = 45°**

Angles in triangle RQS add to 180°, 180° − a = 115°, so d = 180° − 115° − 20° = 45°.

---

4. a | 1 | **n^2**

TIP: You need to recognise common sequences like square and cube numbers.

b | 1 | **$n^2 + 1$**

Each term is 1 more than the square numbers.

c | 1 | **$3n^2$**

Each term is three times the square numbers.

d | 1 | **$2n^2 + 1$**

You get each number by doubling the square numbers and adding 1.

---

5. | 2 |

**(1 mark for the semicircle radius 6 cm and 1 mark for the quarter circle radius 2 cm.
Or 1 mark overall if the right construction is attempted, but not drawn accurately.)**

---

6. a | 1 | **6n + 3**

2n + n + 5 + 3n − 2 = 6n + 3

b | 1 | **2n + 1**

Mean = total ÷ number of servings = (6n + 3) ÷ 3 = 2n + 1.

c | 2 | **10**

2n + 1 = 11, so 2n = 10. **(2 marks for correct answer or 1 mark for using the correct method but getting the wrong answer.)**

---

7. | 3 | $\frac{1}{4}$

Probability of a head on 10p coin is $\frac{2}{3}$. Probability of all heads is $\frac{1}{2} \times \frac{1}{2} \times \frac{2}{3} = \frac{1}{6}$.

Probability of all tails is $\frac{1}{2} \times \frac{1}{2} \times \frac{1}{3} = \frac{1}{12}$. So probability of all the same is $\frac{1}{12} + \frac{1}{6} = \frac{3}{12} = \frac{1}{4}$.

**(3 marks for correct answer, otherwise 1 mark for getting probability of head
(or tail) on 10p coin and 1 mark for getting probabilities of all heads and all tails.)**

---

8. | 2 | **72 kg**

New weight is $\frac{17}{16}$ of old weight. $\frac{1}{16}$ of old weight is 76.5 ÷ 17 = 4.5 kg. Old weight is 4.5 × 16 = 72 kg.

(2 marks for correct answer, otherwise 1 mark for attempting to divide by 17 and multiply by 16.)

---

9. | 2 |

Olivia is 6 months older than Bill	B − 0.5
Mateus is half Bill's age	B + 0.5
Ailsa is 6 months younger than Bill	B + 1
Chris is 1 year older than Bill	0.5B

(1 mark for 1 expression joined correctly, 2 marks for all expressions joined correctly.)

10. a	2	**7x − 15**	$3x − 9 − 6 + 4x = 7x − 15$ **(1 mark for correctly multiplying out without simplifying and 1 mark for simplification.)**
b	2	**$2x^2 − 7x + 3$**	$2x^2 − x − 6x + 3 = 2x^2 − 7x + 3$ **(1 mark for correctly multiplying out without simplifying and 1 mark for simplification.)**

11.	2	**134**	Billie eats $(4 ÷ 7) × 70 = 40$, Anjum eats $(3 ÷ 5) × 40 = 24$, Catie eats 70. $40 + 24 + 70 = 134$. **(2 marks for correct answer, otherwise 1 mark for calculating either Anjum or Billie's total.)**

12. a	1	**0.15 m**	
b	1	**0.00015 m²**	*TIP: Remember: 1 m = 1000 mm, so 1² m² = 1000² mm².*
c	1	**145 mm and 155 mm**	Lower bound = $150 − 5 = 145$ mm. Upper bound = $150 + 5 = 155$ mm.

13. a	1	**0 - 4**	The modal group is the one with the highest frequency.
b	3	**6.5 days**	Use the mid-interval values: $[(2 × 14) + (7 × 8) + (12 × 5) + (17 × 3)] ÷ 30 = 195 ÷ 30 = 6.5$ **(If you get the wrong answer; you can still get 1 mark for multiplying the mid-interval values by the frequencies, and 1 mark for dividing the total by 30.)**
c	1	**Because the mid-interval values are used I the calculation - not the exact values.** **(1 mark for similar comment)**	

14. a	1	**Anna earns £6 per hour, David earns £8 per hour.** Anna marks 3 papers per hour, $3 × 2 = £6$. David marks 4 papers per hour, $4 × 2 = £8$.	
b	3		Some possible points include: (10, 12), (30, 4), (12.5, 9.6) and (22.5, 5.33). The first two are shown on the graph. **(1 mark for points plotted for David & Anna, 1 mark for at least 2 further points, 1 mark for smooth curve.)**

15. a	2	**Right** —	both of them get 20% of the questions right. **(1 mark for right and 1 mark for a suitable explanation.)**
b	2	**Wrong** —	sale price is 90% of original price. New price is 110% of sale price = 110% of 90% = 99%. So new price is not the same as original price. **(1 mark for wrong and 1 mark for a suitable explanation.)**
c	2	**Wrong** —	price in April is 120% of previous price. Price in May is 120% of price in April = 120% of 120% = 144%. That's a 44% rise in two months. **(1 mark for wrong and 1 mark for a suitable explanation.)**

16. a	1	**0.175**	Total no. of sixes = 42, total no. of throws = 240. Estimated probability = $42 ÷ 240 = 0.175$.
b	1	**No, as this is only a little above $\frac{1}{6}$ (0.167) and this is close enough to $\frac{1}{6}$ to suggest that the paper is wrong.** (For 1 mark, must have comparison with 1/6.)	

17. a	1	**$\sqrt{3^2 + 8^2}$**	Using Pythagoras' theorem, EF $= \sqrt{DE^2 + DF^2} = \sqrt{3^2 + 8^2}$
b	2	**3.85 m**	BF $= \sqrt{AF^2 − AB^2} = \sqrt{6^2 − 4.6^2} = \sqrt{36 − 21.16} = \sqrt{14.84} = 3.85$ **(to 3 significant figures)** **(1 mark only for correct working but wrong answer.)**

18.	2	E.g. Any two of: **r = 1, h = 36; r = 2, h = 9; r = 3, h = 4; r = 6, h = 1.** (1 mark for each correct set.)

19.	2	**a = 2 cm, b = 4 cm**	Scale factor of enlargement = AD ÷ AE = $15 ÷ 12 = 1.25$. AC = AB × 1.25 = $8 × 1.25 = 10$, so a = 2 cm. BE = CD ÷ 1.25 = $5 ÷ 1.25 = 4$, so b = 4 cm. **(1 mark for each correct value, otherwise 1 mark overall for some correct working.)**

KS3 Science Paper 1A

Q	Marks	Correct answer	Useful tips
1. a	3	Carbon compounds in fossil fuels like coal, oil and natural gas - C. Decomposers release carbon dioxide into the air - A. Photosynthesis by plants - B. **One mark for each.**	
b	1	Combustion/Burning.	

2. a	1	The amount / volume / mass / weight of the tea / water used.	
b	1	The temperature of the tea.	
c	1	Initial temperature **OR** size / shape of cup **OR** material cup was made from / amount of insulation **OR** time Tim left the cups of tea for **OR** where the cups were left.	

3. a i	1	Solid — C.	
ii	1	Melting — D.	
iii	1	Condensing — F.	*Tip: Subliming, as you might have gathered, is where a substance turns straight from a solid into a gas (or vice versa) without going through the liquid stage. Not many substances do it and you don't really need to know much about it, so don't worry about it too much.*
iv	1	Liquid — A.	
v	1	Freezing — G.	
vi	1	Gas — B.	
vii	1	Boiling — E.	
b	1	Condensing (F) **OR** Freezing (G)	

4. a	2	Light from the lamp shines on the cup and is scattered **OR** reflected. **One mark.** Some of the light travels to Suzanne's eyes and she sees the cup. **One mark.**	
b	2	**The blank boxes of the table should read, 'red — blue' One mark for each.**	
c	1	Black absorbs all light. **OR** It doesn't scatter any light.	
d i	1	30°	
ii	1	30°	
iii	1	2.5 cm	*TIP: Make sure you measure this perpendicular to the mirror — not along the light rays.*
iv	1	2.5 cm	

5. a	3	Zinc — zinc nitrate — nitric acid **[One mark]**. Iron — iron sulfate — sulfuric acid **[One mark]**. Lead — lead chloride — hydrochloric acid **[One mark]**.	
b i	1	E.g. Universal indicator solution **[One mark]**.	
ii	1	E.g. The solution would turn red or orange **[One mark]**.	*Tip: All acids contain hydrogen. Metals like zinc, iron and lead, on the other hand, are pure elements. The only atoms they contain are the metal atoms.*
c	1	The acid.	

6. a	3	A — cell wall **[One mark]**. B — chloroplast **[One mark]**. C — vacuole **[One mark]**.	
b	1	To support the cell.	
c	2	Roots are found underground where there is no light **[One mark]**. They don't need chloroplasts as they don't photosynthesise **[One mark]**.	*Tip: Never make the mistake of thinking that all plant cells have chloroplasts. There's not much point unless the cell photosynthesises, now is there?*

7. a	2	40 × 0.5 = 20 Nm (2000 Ncm) **One mark for answer without unit.**	
b	1	20 ÷ 0.2 = 100 N **Accept answer to (a) ÷ 0.2.**	
c	2	$0.5 \text{ cm}^2 = 0.5 \div 10\ 000 \text{ m}^2$, P = F / A = 80 / 0.00005 = 1 600 000 Pa or Nm^{-2} **[One mark for answer without unit.]** **OR** P = 80 ÷ 0.5 = 160 Ncm^{-2} **[One mark.]**	

8. a	2	Potassium, zinc, nickel, platinum. **(One mark for getting zinc and nickel the wrong way round).**	
b	1	Sodium	
c i	1	Platinum	*TIP: Bleugh, reactivity series. This is <u>hard</u> but you've <u>got</u> to learn it.*
ii	1	Zinc is less reactive than potassium so it does not replace it in the salt.	

Answers

9.	a	2	It damages the cilia, leading to smoker's cough/bronchitis/emphysema [One mark]. It contains carcinogens which cause lung cancer [One mark].
	b	3

Tip: If you're asked to do a graph and you have to come up with the scales for the axes yourself, the rule is that you use as much of the available space as you can. Try not to end up with a tiny graph cramped in one corner of the graph paper. Having said that, it's even more important you pick a sensible scale — don't have each small square being worth 3.25 units or anything silly like that.

[One mark for labelling the axes correctly, one mark for both scales shown correctly on the axes, one mark for showing each bar with the correct height] |
| | c | 1 | Smoking increases the risk of the baby having a smaller birth mass, which can lead to health problems. |

10.	a i	1	Photosynthesis
	ii	1	Oxygen
	iii	1	Carbon dioxide
	iv	1	Respiration
	b	2	There are no insects or other animals to transfer pollen. There is no wind to transfer pollen. **One mark for each.**

11.	a	1	There was a bright flame **OR** ash formed **OR** the magnesium metal turned into white powder.
	b	1	Magnesium oxide.
	c	1	Magnesium + oxygen → magnesium oxide.

12.	a	1	A mixture of compounds.
	b i	1	It is a gas.
	ii	1	Cold water flowing through the condenser cools the naphtha, so it turns back into a liquid.

13.	a	3

[One mark for correctly plotting all the points, one mark for labelling the axes correctly, one mark for a smooth curve through the points similar to that shown] |
| | b | 2 | The rate of photosynthesis / amount of gas/oxygen produced is lower [One mark] the further the lamp is from the plant / the lower the light intensity is [One mark]. |

14.	a i	1	
	ii	1	
	b	1	
	c i	1	Accept 1.7 - 1.9 [One mark]
	ii	1	Accept 33 - 35 [One mark]
	d	1	As the length of the wire increases, the resistance increases [One mark].

KS3 Science Paper 1B

Q	Marks	Correct answer	Useful tips

1. a i | 1 | Water.
ii | 1 | Syrup.
iii | 1 | Sugar.
b | 1 | Heat the mixture **OR** stir the mixture.

Tip: When something dissolves, it hasn't disappeared — its particles have just got so spread out among the particles of solvent that you can't see them any more. So anything that helps them spread out, like stirring or giving them more energy, will help them dissolve.

2. | 5 | Small intestine — absorbs nutrients into the bloodstream **[One mark]**. Stomach — churns up food and mixes it with acid and enzymes **[One mark]**. Teeth — grind up food and mix it with saliva **[One mark]**. Large intestine — absorbs water from the food waste **[One mark]**. Gullet — moves food to the next part of the digestive system by peristalsis **[One mark]**.

3. | 3 |

Description	Letter
An element made up of molecules	B
Molecules in a compound	C
A mixture of different elements	D
An element made up of atoms	A

[Three marks for all correct, one mark for two correct, two marks for three correct]

Tip: If you're still getting mixed up with atoms and compounds and elements and molecules, now's the time to get it all worked out. Molecules are made from more than one atom joined together, and they can be elements (if both atoms are the same) or compounds (if the atoms are of different elements).

4. a i | 1 | Larger than the drag. *[The forward force must be more to make the bike speed up.]*
ii | 1 | Equal to the drag. *[The movement is staying the same so the forces are balanced.]*
iii | 1 | Less than the drag. *[The drag must be more to slow the bike down.]*
b | 1 | Friction

5. a | 2 | Gas A — oxygen **[One mark]**. Gas B — carbon dioxide **[One mark]**.
b | 1 | Respiration.
c | 1 | glucose + oxygen → carbon dioxide + water (+ energy).

6. a | 1 | potassium nitrate
b | 1 | sodium sulfate
c | 1 | calcium chloride

Tip: You need to take the first half of the name of the alkali, and put it with the first half of the name of the acid.

7. a | 2 | Use the same weight of crisps and snack **OR** Use the same amount of; and starting temperature of; water **OR** Keep the same distance of crisp or snack to the test tube. **One mark for any of these up to 2 marks.**
b | 2 | Wear goggles **OR** Point the test tube away from him **OR** Light the food at arms length. **One mark for any 2.**
c | 1 | A. *Because they have a higher energy content.*
d | 1 | Oranges **OR** peas **OR** beans **OR** lemons *Other answers possible.* **One mark for any one of these.**
e i | 1 | Provides a hard substance to clean out the digestive system.
ii | 2 | Lower in fat. Higher in fibre. **One mark for each.**

8. a | 1 | B.
b | 1 | A.
c | 1 | D.
d | 1 | E.
e | 1 | C.

Tip: There's no excuse for mixing up the rock types. Sedimentary rocks are made from sediments — little crumbs of old rock and dead matter that gradually build up into new rock. Metamorphic rocks have metamorphosised (the fancy word for changed) from one type to another. Then all that's left to remember are igneous rocks — they're the, erm, interesting ones, made from volcanoes and lava and stuff.

9. a | 2 | copper sulfate + magnesium → magnesium sulfate + copper **[Lose one mark for each mistake]**.
b | 1 | Because the magnesium takes the place of the copper in the copper sulfate solution, forcing the copper out.
c | 1 | Magnesium. *Tip: Don't get confused — the more reactive element would never be left sitting on its own as a pure metal.*

10.	a	2	When it's summer in England the northern half of the Earth is tilted towards the Sun [One mark], so as the Earth turns, the Sun's rays reach it for more of the day [One mark].
	b	2	Because the Sun's rays are spread over a small area of land [One mark] so the energy is focused on a small area and the land gets warm [One mark].

11.	a	1	The concentration of the acid [One mark].
	b	2	Any two of: the volume of acid / mass of marble chips / the size/surface area of the marble chips [Two marks].
	c	1	Repeat her experiment and take an average of the results [One mark].
	d i	3	[One mark for numbering and labelling the axes correctly, one mark for plotting the points correctly, one mark for joining the points with a smooth curve]
	ii	1	E.g. the mass of the beaker and contents decreases for 20 minutes and then stays the same [One mark].
	iii	1	18½ minutes. *The mass was still changing after 15 minutes, but had stopped by 20, meaning the reaction had finished.*
	iv	2	250.0 – 239.5 = 10.5 g. [One mark for correct answer, one mark for correct unit]

12.	a	2	If only red and blue light shine on the dress, it absorbs the blue light [One mark] and reflects only the red light and so appears red [One mark].
	b	2	Yellow light is made up of red and green light [One mark]. When both red and green light are shining on it, the dress reflects both colours and appears yellow [One mark].
	c	1	Yellow.

13.	a	2	One muscle contracts to bend the joint [One mark] and the other contracts to straighten the joint [One mark].
	b	1	A

14.	a	1	The arrow should be drawn pointing directly upwards from the sliding bolt, towards the electromagnet.
	b	1	Gravity.
	c	1	iron **OR** steel **OR** nickel **OR** cobalt.
	d	1	Use a higher voltage/current/more powerful battery **OR** have more turns in the coil of wire of the electromagnet **OR** use a better (more easily magnetised) material for the core of the electromagnet.

15.	a	3	[Take away one mark for each mistake or omission]
	b	1	There are many variables that cannot be controlled when working in the field [One mark].
	c	1	By counting the number of slugs and snails using a quadrat. [One mark]
	d	2	The number of blue tits will decrease [One mark], as there will be less food/fewer slugs and snails for them [One mark].

KS3 Science Paper 2A

Q	Marks	Correct answer	Useful tips
1.	3	Muscle — tissue [One mark]. Heart **AND** Brain — organ [One mark]. Sperm **AND** Neurone — cell [One mark].	
2. a	4	A — stomach, B — large intestine **OR** colon, C — small intestine, D — anus **OR** rectum [One mark for each correct answer].	
b	1	Many food molecules are too big to be absorbed into the bloodstream/can't pass through the gut wall.	
3. a	1	Sedimentary	
b	1	Metamorphic	
c	1	Igneous	
4. a	1	DNA	
b	1	Sperm.	
c	1	Nuclei **OR** Nucleus **OR** Chromosomes	
d	1	Inherit.	
5. a	1	Distillation	
b	1	100 °C	
c	1	It condenses the water vapour.	
d	4	1 Condensing 2 Boiling **OR** Evaporating 3 Melting 4 Freezing	
e	1	*in piece of apparatus labelled X* 1 *in the flask containing impure water* 2 **Both required for one mark.**	

Q	Marks	Correct answer	
6. a	1	conduction	
b	3	Your graph should look similar to →	
c	2	She could use metal blocks made of different metals (but of the same mass) [One mark]. She would need to calculate the change in temperature over time [One mark].	[One mark for a sensible scale and correctly-labelled axes, one mark for correctly plotting all the points, one mark for good line of best fit.]
d	1	Accept 55 °C - 57 °C.	
e	1	It is easier to see the trend.	

Q	Marks	Correct answer	Useful tips
7. a	1	The ice melted.	*Tip:* So, kinetic energy stores. Sounds a bit technical, but it's simple really. All particles move about a bit — even in solids they vibrate, and in gases they rush about like crazy. When something warms up, the energy in its particles' kinetic energy stores increases. When something cools down, the energy decreases. That's why solids tend to be quite stiff and dense, and gases are floaty and, well, mainly empty space.
b	1	Energy in their kinetic energy stores increased.	
c	1	Energy in their kinetic energy stores decreased.	
d	1	10 °C	
e	1	20 °C	
8. a	1	kinetic	
b	1	The wind energy is free **OR** it causes less environmental problems/pollution than electricity produced by burning fossil fuels **OR** it uses a renewable energy resource.	
c	1	Any one of: it's less reliable because the wind doesn't always blow, it spoils the view, it is noisy, there is a low energy output, it is expensive to build.	
d	1	The Sun.	

Answers

9.	a	1	A and Y
	b	1	It is made of a mixture of substance A or Y and substance B.
	c	1	An ink line would be separated out by the solvent and make the chromatogram unclear.
	d	1	If it was below the surface the substances would wash out into the solvent instead of moving up the paper.

10.	a i	1	20 kWh
	ii	1	240p **OR** £2.40
	b i	1	0.3 kWh
	ii	1	3.5 hours

11.	a	3	E.g. [Circuit complete for one mark, lamps connected in parallel for one mark, switches to isolate the lamps independently for one mark.]
	b	2	The battery might run out more quickly / need replacing more often [One mark] because more energy would be needed to power both the lamps [One mark].

12.	a	1	magnesium + water → magnesium oxide + hydrogen
	b i	2	potassium + water → potassium hydroxide [One mark] + hydrogen [One mark].
	ii	1	alkali
	ii	1	pH 12

13.	a	1	Filtration
	b	1	As a control **OR** To show it's the dissolved substances that affect it
	c i	1	Minerals **OR** salts **OR** nutrients
	ii	1	Root hairs **OR** Large surface area **OR** They spread out
	d	1	The leaves need light for photosynthesis.

14.	a	1	A
	b	1	C
	c	1	B *Tip: Remember, air resistance isn't a fixed thing. It changes depending on how fast you're going and how big you are.*
	d	1	C
	e	2	speed = distance ÷ time = 100 ÷ 15 = 6.7 m/s [Correct answer for one mark, correct unit for one mark.]

15.	a	2	Tablet B [One mark]. Because it neutralised more acid than tablet A [One mark].
	b	2	Any two of: e.g. strength/concentration of acid / volume of drops / temperature [One mark each].
	c	1	Type of tablet
	d	1	He could repeat the experiment and calculate an average.

KS3 Science Paper 2B

Q	Marks	Correct answer	Useful tips

1. a | 3 | Copper — 1 [One mark]. Sulfur — 1 [One mark]. Oxygen — 4 [One mark].

b | 1 | Copper sulfate. *Tip: If you've recognised the copper, the sulfur and the oxygen, the name of the salt should be pretty obvious.*

2. a | 2 | E.g.

[One mark for a straight line from any point on the child to the mirror, a straight line from the top mirror to the bottom mirror and a straight line from the mirror to the driver's eye, one mark for direction of light going from child to driver.]

Tip: Of course, there are other rays of light bouncing off every bit of the child he can see. Luckily you only have to show one of them — otherwise things would get very complicated.

b | 2 | light ray / reflector

[One mark for showing that the light is reflected onto the opposite surface. One mark for showing that it is then reflected back in the direction from which it originally came.]

3. a | 2 | Nucleus — controls the cell. Cytoplasm — where all the chemical reactions take place. Cell membrane — controls what passes into and out of the cell. [One correct for one mark, all correct for two marks.]

b i | 1 | Respiration.

ii | 3 | Oxygen — used [One mark]. Glucose — used [One mark]. Carbon dioxide — made [One mark].

iii | 1 | Diffusion

4. a | 3 | E.g.

[Two marks if all points are plotted correctly, one mark if four or more points are plotted correctly. One mark for straight line of best fit]

b | 1 | D

c | 1 | Accept any answer between 6 and 8.

5. a | 2 | It is repelled by magnet A [One mark], so moves downwards away from it [One mark].

b | 2 | If it's the wrong way up it will attract the small magnet [One mark], which will move in the wrong direction and give a result that's off the scale [One mark].

c | 1 | So that the arm is balanced before any magnets are tested **OR** to increase the sensitivity / accuracy / precision of the pointer / so that the pointer moves more.

d | 1 | The stronger magnet will give a bigger reading / make the pointer move further up the scale.

6. a | 2 | The water has become more acidic [One mark], because the universal indicator has turned from green (neutral) to orange (weak acid) [One mark].

b | 2 | Ordinary air didn't affect the pH of the water after 2 minutes [One mark], because the universal indicator stayed green (neutral) [One mark].

c | 2 | Becky's experiment showed that breathing into water made it more acidic [One mark], and Huang's showed that this was due to a substance in her breath and not just due to air bubbling through it [One mark].

7. a | 1 | diaphragm

b | 1 | Because the volume of the jar has increased/the pressure in the jar has decreased.

Answers

c	2	The balloons would deflate [One mark], because the volume of the jar has decreased/the pressure in the jar has increased [One mark].	
d	1	E.g. tar	

8. a	2	Rock B [One mark], because its crystals are bigger due to it cooling more slowly/underground [One mark].	
b	2	Marble — metamorphic. Limestone — sedimentary. Granite — igneous. [One mark one correct, two marks for all].	

9. a	1	friction **OR** air resistance
b	2	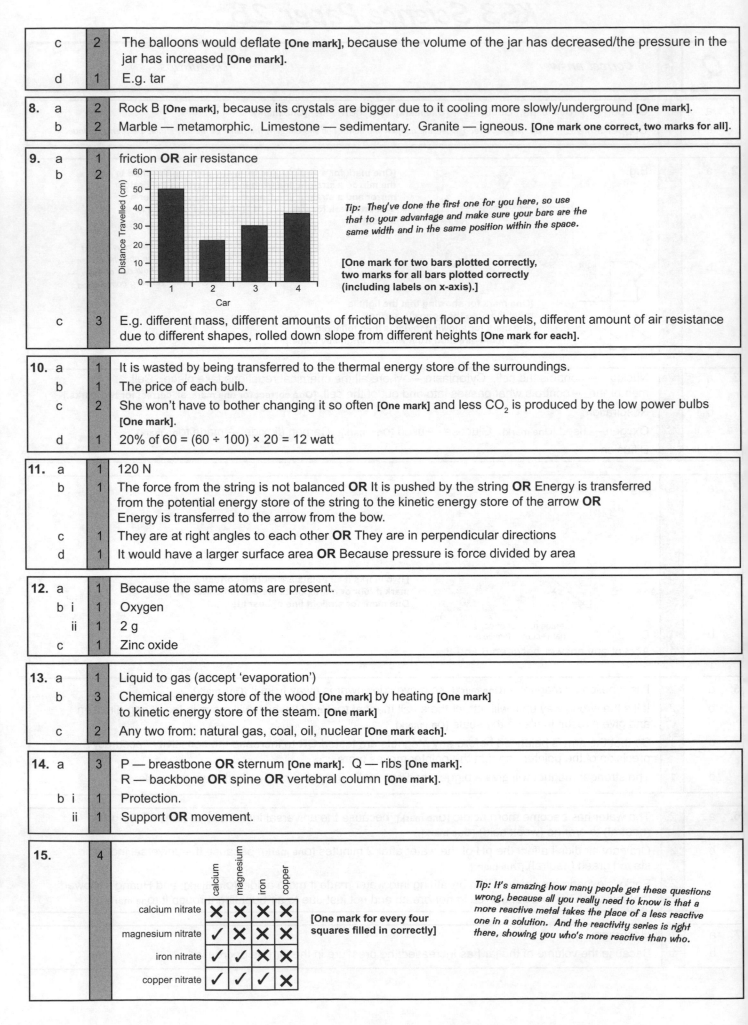 *Tip: They've done the first one for you here, so use that to your advantage and make sure your bars are the same width and in the same position within the space.* [One mark for two bars plotted correctly, two marks for all bars plotted correctly (including labels on x-axis).]
c	3	E.g. different mass, different amounts of friction between floor and wheels, different amount of air resistance due to different shapes, rolled down slope from different heights [One mark for each].

10. a	1	It is wasted by being transferred to the thermal energy store of the surroundings.
b	1	The price of each bulb.
c	2	She won't have to bother changing it so often [One mark] and less CO_2 is produced by the low power bulbs [One mark].
d	1	20% of 60 = (60 ÷ 100) × 20 = 12 watt

11. a	1	120 N
b	1	The force from the string is not balanced **OR** It is pushed by the string **OR** Energy is transferred from the potential energy store of the string to the kinetic energy store of the arrow **OR** Energy is transferred to the arrow from the bow.
c	1	They are at right angles to each other **OR** They are in perpendicular directions
d	1	It would have a larger surface area **OR** Because pressure is force divided by area

12. a	1	Because the same atoms are present.
b i	1	Oxygen
ii	1	2 g
c	1	Zinc oxide

13. a	1	Liquid to gas (accept 'evaporation')
b	3	Chemical energy store of the wood [One mark] by heating [One mark] to kinetic energy store of the steam. [One mark]
c	2	Any two from: natural gas, coal, oil, nuclear [One mark each].

14. a	3	P — breastbone **OR** sternum [One mark]. Q — ribs [One mark]. R — backbone **OR** spine **OR** vertebral column [One mark].
b i	1	Protection.
ii	1	Support **OR** movement.

15.	4	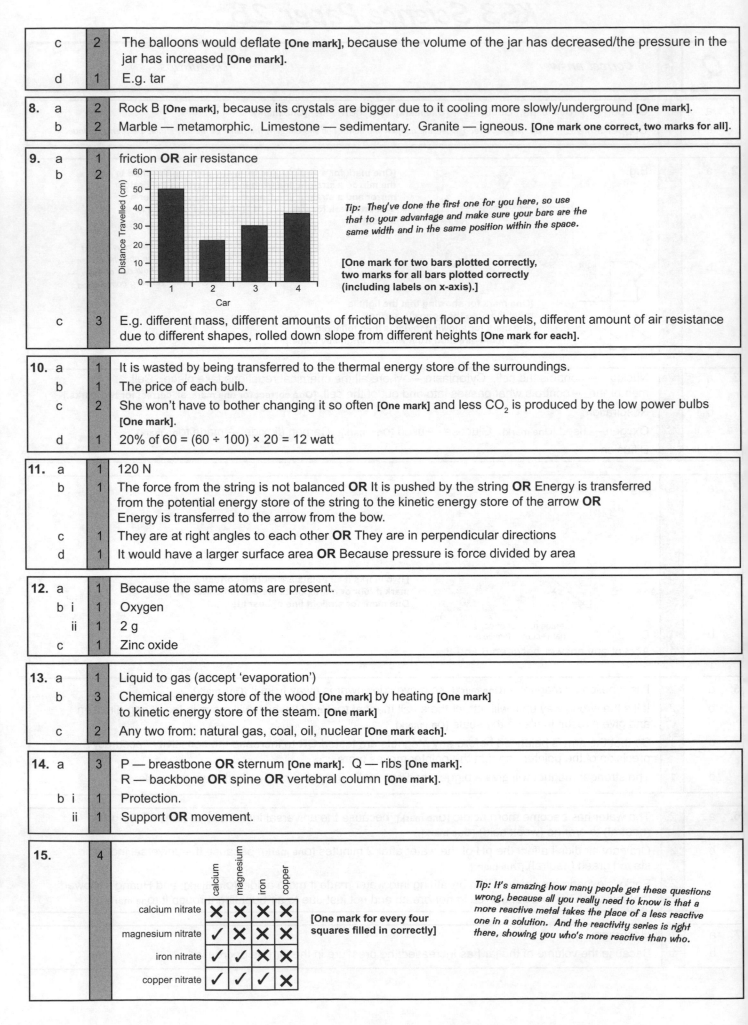 [One mark for every four squares filled in correctly] *Tip: It's amazing how many people get these questions wrong, because all you really need to know is that a more reactive metal takes the place of a less reactive one in a solution. And the reactivity series is right there, showing you who's more reactive than who.*

KS3 Science Paper 3A

Q	Marks	Correct answer	Useful tips
1. a	1	Lamp **OR** bulb.	
b	1	Ammeter.	
c	1	Battery/Cell.	
d	1	Voltmeter.	

2.	4	Stomach acid — red — 1 [One mark]. Soap powder — blue — 10 [One mark]. Lemon juice — orange — 3 [One mark]. Salt water — green — 7 [One mark].	

3. a	4	**A** - sperm tube, **B** - penis, **C** - urethra, **D** - testis, **E** - bladder [All correct for four marks, two correct for one mark, three correct for two marks, four correct for three marks]	
b	1	Sperm	

4. a	2	96 Nm [One mark for 96, one mark for Nm (OR can be 9600 Ncm)]	**TIPS:** Moments and energy transfer in all their glory in one question. So make sure you've got the answers right. If not practise and practise again and again.
b	2	12 m/s [One mark for 12, one mark for m/s (OR can be 1200 cm/s)]	
c	1	300 Hz [No mark if more than one frequency circled]	
d	1	chemical energy store of the bell-ringer (No mark for 'energy in the bell-ringer')	
	1	transferred mechanically **OR** transferred to the bell **OR** transferred from the rope **OR** to the rope **OR** the kinetic energy store of the bell	
	1	as bell swings, energy from the bell's kinetic energy store is transferred to its gravitational potential energy store (No mark for if the bell swinging is not mentioned)	
	1	transferred away by sound **OR** transferred to surroundings/the air/people's ears	
		[One mark for each of the four potential points with a maximum of 3 marks. The points must be made in a logical order.]	

5. a	2	From top to bottom, the column should read: 20, 24, 29, 21, 28 (Lose one mark for each mistake)	
b	2	Any two of: always use the same mass of cornflakes, always use the same volume of water, keep the boiling tube the same distance from the burning cornflakes, keep the thermometer at the same height in the boiling tube [One mark each].	
c	1	They could repeat the experiment several times and take an average.	
d	1	They could insulate the apparatus **OR** use a wider-bottomed container for the water (to absorb more of the heat from the cornflakes).	

6. a	1	Distillation.	
b	1	They have different boiling points **OR** alcohol boils at a lower temperature than water does.	
c	1	The alcohol is cooling and turning back into a liquid / condensing.	
d	2	Brandy [One mark], because the alcohol in the wine evaporates off first and runs into the container of brandy [One mark].	

7. a	1	Attrition **OR** Erosion. [One mark for each]	**TIPS:** All this stuff about rocks might seem like geography, but it's a very popular science question.
b	2	They are smoothed and rounded. They get smaller. [One mark for each]	
c	1	Stage 4: Deposition / Sedimentation.	
	1	Stage 5: Compression/Compaction.	

8.	a i	2	Plastic **OR** wood [One mark], because it is not a good conductor of energy so will stop his hand being burnt [One mark].
	ii	2	Copper **OR** steel [One mark], because it has a high melting point **OR** because it is not flammable [One mark].
	b	1	The smoke is hotter than the air in the room, meaning it is less dense, so it rises — straight up the chimney.
	c	1	The energy is transferred by radiation.

Tip: That's right, there was more than one correct answer. That might happen now and again, so don't let it confuse you — don't sit there for hours trying to come up with a reason why wood wouldn't be any good as a handle.

9.	a	1	Any one of: wear goggles, use a heat-proof mat, handle the hot crucible with tongs [One mark].
	b	2	Element: 1 **OR** 2 [One mark]. Compound: 4 [One mark].
	c i	1	Iron sulfide.
	ii	1	FeS.
	d	1	8.8 g.

10.	a i	2	CO_2 **OR** H_2O **OR** CO **OR** C. One mark for any of these up to 2 marks.
	ii	2	Water droplets on the jar **OR** Soot **OR** Energy released. One mark for any of these up to 2 marks.
	b i	2	The carbon dioxide level decreases. The oxygen level rises.
	ii	2	Photosynthesis stops. Respiration continues **OR** The changes would reverse. [One mark for each.]
	c i	1	Chloroplasts.
	ii	1	Nucleus.

TIPS: If you find you're running out of time in these practice papers think about how long you spend on each question. Don't spend ages on one question, especially if it's only worth a mark or two. Get on with the rest and come back to it later.

11.	a	2	The turbine transfers energy from the wind's kinetic energy store to the kinetic energy store of the turbine. [One mark]. This energy is transferred to the kinetic energy store of the generator [One mark].
	b	1	The wind can not be used up.
	c	1	Tidal energy **OR** Solar power **OR** Biomass **OR** Hydroelectric **OR** Geothermal. [One mark for any one of these.]

12.	a	2	Any two from: rabbit, mouse, sparrow [One mark each].
	b	2	Any two from: fox, weasel, buzzard [One mark each].
	c	1	The Sun.
	d i	1	Weasel numbers would drop because they would have less food [One mark]. (No mark if the answer suggests the weasels die.)
	ii	1	The number of mice would go up because there would be more food for them **OR** because there are now fewer weasels **OR** mouse numbers would drop because the weasels would eat more of them now that there are no rabbits [One mark] (Mark only awarded if the reason explains the effect on numbers. The mark can also be awarded if the same answer concludes that mouse numbers would stay the same overall.)

| 13. | | 2 | The elephant's weight is spread out over a much bigger area [One mark], so it exerts less pressure on the floor than Mrs Lightfoot's heels which cover a much smaller area [One mark]. |

| 14. | a | 1 | 800 × 10 = 8000 N. |
| | b | 2 | Pressure = force ÷ area. Pressure = 8000 ÷ 0.25 = 32 000 N/m² [One mark for correct answer, one mark for correct units] |

KS3 Science Paper 3B

Q	Marks	Correct answer	Useful tips

---

1. | **3** | Team A pulls with a total force of 27 N + 24 N + 21 N = 72 N **[One mark].**
Team B pulls with a total force of 19 N + 32 N + 23 N = 74 N **[One mark].**
So team B will win (because they pull with a greater total force) **[One mark].**

Tip: Dead simple this — to find the total force in any direction, just add all the forces going that way together.

---

2. a | **1** | 'It affects the nervous system.' **should be circled.**

b i | **2** | The chance of having an accident increases, the rate of increase gets faster the more alcohol is in the blood.
One mark for just saying 'it increases'.

ii | **1** | 'Alcohol increases the time it takes for a person to react'. **should be circled.**

---

3. a | **3** |

Nucleus

Cell Membrane

Cytoplasm   **[One mark for each]**

b | **2** | Cell wall **OR** Vacuole **OR** Chloroplasts. **[One mark for any of these up to 2 marks]**

c | **1** | Tissue **OR** organ

---

4. a | **1** | Oxygen.

b | **1** | Oxygen.

c | **1** | 6 + 12 + 6 = 24.

---

5. a | **3** |

Distance fallen by marble (cm) vs Time taken (s)

[One mark for sensible scale on axes, one mark for correctly plotting points, one mark for good line of best fit]

Tip: Don't worry if you didn't give the actual speed of the marble. There's only one mark for the question and they didn't ask you to calculate anything, so saying the speed is constant should be fine. Well done if you did work it out though. Smarty-pants.

b | **1** | They show that the marble falls at a constant speed (of 5 cm/s).

---

6. a | **3** | Hydrochloric acid — calcium chloride — calcium hydroxide **[One mark].** Sulfuric acid — copper sulfate — copper hydroxide **[One mark].** Nitric acid — iron nitrate — iron hydroxide **[One mark].**

b | **1** | Hydrochloric acid.

c | **1** | Nitric acid.

---

7. a | **2** | From the chemical energy store of Matt's muscles **[One mark]**
to the kinetic energy stores of the air/gas particles **[One mark].**

b | **1** | The molecules hit the walls of the balloon **OR** they bounce off the walls/balloon

c | **1** | They speed up/get faster

d | **1** | They'll hit the wall of the balloon more often/harder/faster **OR** more collisions with balloon
No mark for 'more collisions' or 'molecules move faster'

Answers

8.	a	2	Methane + oxygen $\rightarrow$ carbon dioxide + water [Take away one mark for each mistake or omission].
	b	2	More carbon dioxide [One mark] and less oxygen [One mark].
	c	1	C.

Tip: Any compound of just hydrogen and carbon produces water and carbon dioxide when it burns.

9.	a	3	20 Nm. *100 × 0.2 = 20 Nm.* [One mark for working, one for units, one for answer.]
	b i	1	20 Nm. *(It balances the moment of the 100 N force.)*
	ii	1	25 N. *20 ÷ 0.8 = 25 N.*
	iii	2	20 N/cm². *100 ÷ 5 = 20 N/cm².* [One mark for units, one for answer.]

TIPS: When you do these mathsy questions you've got to remember the units.

10.	a	1	Carbon dioxide + water $\rightarrow$ glucose + oxygen.
	b	1	By counting the number of bubbles produced in a given time.
	c	1	Repeat the experiment and take an average of his readings.
	d	1	Chlorophyll.
	e	1	By light.

11.	a	4	P — ovary [One mark]. Q — oviduct **OR** Fallopian tube [One mark]. R — uterus **OR** womb [One mark]. S — cervix [One mark].
	b	1	An ovary.
	c	1	Day 14.
	d	1	Its lining thickens.

| 12. | a | 3 | Similar to: |

[One mark for showing the direction of the ray changing correctly, one mark for showing that the ray spreads out, one mark for giving a spectrum of colours]

| 12. | b | 2 | Dispersion [One mark] and refraction [One mark]. |

13.	a	2	Heating the coin gives the particles more energy, so they vibrate more strongly [One mark]. This means that each particle takes up a slightly bigger volume, so the coin expands [One mark].
	b	2	The particles of rose-water had more energy after heating [One mark], so they turned into gas particles (which could spread around the room) more readily [One mark].
	c	2	They both involve the particles of the substances [One mark] changing their behaviour after being given more energy [One mark].

| 14. | a | 2 | Lit: A, B [One mark]. Not lit: C, D [One mark]. |
| | b | 3 | Close switch S1 [One mark]. Open switch S2 [One mark]. Remove the voltmeter **OR** connect the voltmeter in parallel not in series [One mark]. |

15.	a	2	By evaporating all the water [One mark] to see if a solid is left behind (because KCl will only be left if it was dissolved in the water) [One mark].
	b	1	There was no reaction because potassium is more reactive than magnesium.
	c	2	A secondary source [One mark] because their conclusions are based on an error [One mark].

How to Mark the English Papers

It's pretty straightforward. You can mark all the papers using the mark schemes on the next few pages. Ask an adult to mark them for you if you like — it's good to get someone else's opinion of your work.

There are **lots** of good ways to answer every single one of the questions in these practice papers. That means we can't tell you **word for word** what your answer should be.

Instead we've given a description of the **kind** of answer that'll get you a certain number of marks. It might look a bit complicated, but once you get stuck in, it should all become clear.

Reading Paper

*   Mark the **Reading** questions just for reading comprehension. Don't knock off marks for badly written answers, or give more marks for well written ones.

*   Tot up the marks to get a score out of **32**.

Writing Paper

*   This is marked for **sentence structure and punctuation**, **text structure and organisation** and **composition and effect**.

*   Add up the separate marks for each task to get a mark out of **50**.

Shakespeare Paper

*   The Shakespeare question is only marked for **understanding** — there are no marks for the written style.

*   The Shakespeare question is marked out of **18**.

Using the Mark Schemes for the Writing Paper

*   Read the work and then look at the **mark scheme tables** for each question. Decide which of the "What's the Answer Like?" descriptions matches it **most closely**.

*   Each description gives a **range** of possible marks. If the answer does **every single thing** in one particular description, and does them well, give it a mark from the top end of the range. If the answer **doesn't** do everything in the description, but does do **some of it**, give it a mark from the bottom of the range.

*   And obviously, the longest answers aren't necessarily the best ones.

Set A — Reading Paper

There are some really helpful points about marking
on page 293 — make sure you read them first.

1. 1 mark for an answer which gives all three abilities:
    - fly
    - drink blood
    - run / sprint

2. 1 mark for any valid explanation, e.g.
    - He uses an exclamation mark to make it sound like something dramatic has happened.
    - He uses a slang word "Yikes" to amuse us and encourage us to think we'll understand the article.

3. 2 marks for a clear explanation, including a quotation, e.g.
    - He starts paragraph 6 with the phrase "Thing is," which expresses a reservation about what has gone before.
    - He repeats the words "small animals," which shows that the two paragraphs have a subject in common.

4a. 1 mark for a valid phrase, e.g.
    - "fleet-footed"
    - "sprint along the ground"
    - "break into a loping run"

4b. 1 mark for the word "lumbering"

5. A good answer is likely to cover points like the high number of quotes, use of comparisons (e.g. "flop around like fish out of water" or "It's as if they were designed to chase race cars…"), mixing of scientific quotes with simple explanations (e.g. "You might want to jog across the room… to understand what that means") and the way subheadings identify section topics.

    1 or 2 marks for an explanation that recognises that the tone is light-hearted and picks out some examples but does not cover all three prompts.

    3 marks for an explanation that comments on the effects of specific details and quotations but does not cover all three prompts in detail.

    4 or 5 marks for a detailed answer in which all three prompts are dealt with and comments are supported with appropriate quotations and explanations.

6. 1 mark for a valid answer, e.g.
    - He writes as though he is talking directly to the reader in chatty, informal language.
    - He uses multiple exclamation marks to show excitement about the topic.
    - He describes a grotesque and humorous scene from a film.

7. 1 mark for a valid answer, e.g.
    - The book explores important themes (such as family, friendship, making sacrifices).

8. 1 mark for the point that it should contain shocking, thrilling, action-packed, violent events.

    1 mark for the point that it should contain more subtle moments that make the reader think and brood.

9. A good explanation might cover the enduring nature of his enthusiasm e.g. "That thirst for 'more' has never left me"; the range and type of emotions triggered by horror stories, e.g. it "explores" themes, "lingers" in the mind and contrasts "the subtle menace between the sudden bursts of action and violence"; the effect of single and multiple exclamation marks, and the unsettling effect of ellipses ("...") in paragraph 5.

    1 or 2 marks for general comments which recognise Shan's enjoyment of reading and writing horror. There will be some reference to the text but some of the prompts may not be covered.

    3 marks for an answer that comments on the effects of specific details and quotations. Some of the prompts may not be covered in detail.

    4 or 5 marks for a detailed answer in which all three prompts are dealt with and comments are supported with appropriate quotations and explanations.

10. 1 mark for a valid answer, e.g.
    - He saw everything by "moonlight."
    - "a breath of fresh air, though it were of the night" — he is describing night air.
    - "this nocturnal existence" — he is making it clear that he only moves around at night.

11. 1 mark for each row completed, to a maximum of 2 marks. **Must include a valid quotation** and an explanation e.g.
    - "I felt that I was indeed in prison" — He feels trapped.
    - "It is destroying my nerve" — He is starting to get jumpy and scared.
    - "there is ground for my terrible fear in this accursed place" — He is convinced that the castle is dangerous.

Set A — Reading Paper

There are some really helpful points about marking on page 293— make sure you read them first.

12a. 1 mark for a valid description of a feeling and 1 mark for a supporting quotation, e.g. he's beginning to relax as he looks at the beautiful landscape — "there was peace and comfort in every breath I drew."

12b. 1 mark for a valid description of a feeling and 1 mark for a supporting quotation, e.g. he is disgusted and frightened by the strange sight of the Count — "my very feelings changed to repulsion and terror".

13. 1 mark for a valid answer — must include an example with an explanation, e.g.

- "I am in fear, in awful fear" — repeating the word fear emphasises how extreme his emotion is.
- "What manner of man is this, or what manner of creature" — repeating the word "manner" shows how uncertain he is about the creature he can see.

14. 1 mark for each valid explanation in the "Effect on the reader" column, up to a maximum of 4 marks, e.g.

For *"Hopping is good…roll over and squash a bat"*

- "slurping" makes the bat sound comical.
- The idea of it being squashed makes it seem more vulnerable.

For *"the clever little mammals…"*

- The phrase "little mammals" makes them sound endearing.
- Calling them "clever little mammals" suggests that we could admire the bats, not fear them.

For *"down the castle wall…like great wings"*

- The description of the Count above the "dreadful abyss" makes him sound confident and frightening.
- The words "like great wings" emphasise his power and strangeness.

For *"what manner of creature is it…"*

- Imprecise words like "manner" and "semblance" create a feeling of mystery about who or what the Count is.
- The use of a question helps emphasise the narrator's confusion to the reader.

Set B — Reading Paper

*There are some really helpful points about marking
on page 293— make sure you read them first.*

1. 1 mark for any valid answer e.g.
    - It was because things kept moving around, e.g. the people in the portraits.

2a. 1 mark for any one of the following phrases:
    - "He would drop waste-paper baskets on your head"
    - "pull rugs from under your feet"
    - "pelt you with bits of chalk"
    - "sneak up behind you, invisible, grab your nose"

2b. 1 mark for a reasonable explanation e.g.
    - The list shows he's unpleasant in many ways.
    - The list emphasises how unpleasant he is.

3. 1 mark for a valid example e.g.
    - Doors that won't open unless you ask them politely or tickle them in the right place.
    - The poltergeist Peeves drops waste-paper baskets on people's heads.

    1 mark for a valid explanation e.g.
    - The humour is quirky and surprising.
    - The description has a slapstick humour, like a cartoon.

4. Ideas for answering this question include the writer's use of descriptive language, her matter-of-fact telling of magical events and the way her characters have adapted to them in practical ways.

    1 or 2 marks for a simple answer that attempts to answer the question but doesn't cover all three of the prompts.

    3 marks for an answer that covers all three prompts but isn't developed.

    4 or 5 marks for an answer that covers all three prompts, is clear and detailed and has points supported with quotations.

5. 1 mark for any valid technique, e.g.
    - first paragraph is printed in bold
    - short sentences
    - repetition
    - emotive language

    1 mark for a valid explanation, e.g.
    - Short sentences stop the reader from becoming bored.
    - Repetition makes the reader curious about what is coming next.
    - Emotive language makes the reader care about what is happening.

6. 1 mark for a valid impression, 1 further mark for a supporting quotation, e.g.
    - It's imposing — "the grand double door".
    - It's got lots of facilities — "there is a work room, kitchen, common room and the sofa room."

7. 1 mark for each row of the table completed with a valid description of how that aspect of the article helps the reader.

    Example answers for "Sections describing different pupils' experiences":
    - They show the reader different points of view.
    - They help the reader remember what it felt like to start a new school.

    Example answers for "Headline and subheadings":
    - They make it clear what the article and different sections are about.
    - They divide the article up so that it isn't so daunting.

8. Answers for this question could comment on the excitement expressed by all three students, the use of direct questions in the introduction to make the reader think about their own experience and the use of the headmaster's comment to make general rather than specific statements.

    1 or 2 marks for a simple answer that attempts to address some but not all of the prompts.

    3 marks for an answer that attempts to address all three prompts but isn't detailed or doesn't use quotations to support ideas.

    4 or 5 marks for an answer that clearly addresses all three prompts and answers the question using quotations or examples from the text.

9. 1 mark for a valid comment e.g.
    - It seemed tough but happy.
    - It sounds unpleasant and difficult.

    1 further mark for a relevant supporting quotation e.g.
    - "Despite these conditions, Cherry-Anne and Lisbeth have happy memories..."
    - "The schoolroom was crowded, dark and cold".

10. 1 mark for any valid example, e.g.
    - The boys "were each given one stroke with the cane on the hand".

Set B — Reading Paper

There are some really helpful points about marking on page 293— make sure you read them first.

11. 1 mark for any reasonable suggestion, e.g.

   • The logbook entries make the story more interesting.

   • The logbook entries help us understand the day-to-day running of the school more clearly.

12. 1 mark for each valid quotation and explanation, up to a maximum of 3 marks, e.g.

   • "hanging war issue blankets from the ceiling" — gives the reader the idea that materials were basic and that the school staff were doing their best with limited resources.

   • "did little to stop the noise" — emphasises to the reader how cramped the conditions were.

   • "stop the heat from … reaching the far end" — makes the reader feel sorry for the children.

   • "had to wear her outdoor coat all day to keep warm" — makes the reader empathise with Lisbeth by describing how she coped with the difficult conditions.

13. 1 mark for an appropriate choice for the purpose of the text, and 1 mark for a valid explanation. Up to a maximum of 4 marks, e.g.

	Wingrave School	Harry Potter and the Philosopher's Stone
Purpose of the text (circle your answer)	entertaining ⟨informing⟩ persuading	⟨entertaining⟩ informing persuading
Give a reason for your choice	The text uses lots of factual, real-life detail about evacuation, e.g. the number of children evacuated from Tufnell Park in London.	The text uses entertaining humour to describe the school, e.g. portraits that keep going to visit each other.

Set C — Reading Paper

*There are some really helpful points about marking
on page 293— make sure you read them first.*

1. 1 mark for any valid phrase, e.g.
    * "Let there be none to mark"
    * "Rest in the woodland free"
    * "the loveliness bold / Loneliest landscapes wear"

2. 1 mark for each simile, up to a maximum of 2 marks:
    * "Bright as the heavens above"
    * "Fresh as the wild bush flowers"

3. a) 1 mark: "Give us"

    b) 1 mark for any reasonable explanation, e.g.
    * It links the first three verses.
    * It makes the poem sound like a prayer.
    * It makes the reader feel like part of the poem.

4. 1 or 2 marks for an explanation which: picks out some relevant examples in response to the prompts; does **not** cover all three prompts; makes very simple comments in response to the prompts; does not explicitly tackle the question of how the poet builds up a picture of the bush.

    3 marks for an explanation which: picks out and explains examples relevant to all three prompts, giving a basic overview of how the poet builds up a picture of the bush.

    4 or 5 marks for an explanation which: explicitly explores how the writer creates a picture of the bush; picks out and explains examples of all three prompts.

5. 1 mark for any valid phrase, e.g.
    * "biggest challenge of my life so far"
    * "no-one would turn their back on this chance"

6. 1 mark for any valid phrase up to a maximum of 1 mark, e.g.
    * steep landscape
    * land flattened out
    * grey flint lake
    * greenery was sparse.

7. 1 mark for each explanation **backed up with a quotation** up to a maximum of 3 marks, e.g.
    * contrast between the rock climb and the "relative comfort of the lake side"
    * emphasising how hard it is with phrases like "it wasn't possible to make out any kind of route"
    * short sentences like "The ropes were uncoiled and the harness was on"
    * explaining how vulnerable she felt with phrases like "it might not stop me being injured in a serious fall"

8. ½ mark for each factual answer drawn from the text, up to a maximum of 2 marks, e.g.
    * You can attach the rope to the top of the cliff for short climbs.
    * Make sure ropes are clean and dry when put away.
    * Coil ropes carefully.
    * You climb in pairs.

9. 1 or 2 marks for an explanation which: picks out some relevant examples in response to the prompts; does **not** cover all three prompts; makes very simple comments in response to the prompts, which do not engage with the climber's experience.

    3 marks for an explanation which: picks out and explains examples relevant to all three prompts, giving a basic overview of how the writer conveys her feelings to the reader.

    4 or 5 marks for an explanation which: explicitly explores how the writer conveys her feelings to the reader; picks out and explains examples of all three prompts.

10. ½ mark for each appropriate word/phrase up to a maximum of 1 mark, e.g.
    * "the speediest" • "sexiest" • "snatched"
    * "hot off his wheels" • "under the handlebars".

Set C — Reading Paper

There are some really helpful points about marking on page 293 — make sure you read them first.

11. 1 mark for each relevant quotation **with explanation** (maximum 2 marks), e.g.
- "I didn't really think about it on the way round" — shows he is committed to racing and concentrates hard when riding.
- "I just had to focus on getting round" — shows concentration.
- "I think you've got to be ready to ride in anything" shows commitment whatever the weather.
- "You should be training in all weathers" shows he is prepared to put in the hard work.

12. 1 mark for each quotation **with explanation** that answers the question (maximum 2 marks), e.g.
- "I knew I was making good time" — shows Andrew is confident.
- "it's easy to blame the mud" — he doesn't think much of people who make excuses.
- "you've got to be ready to ride in anything" — shows Andrew is tough and dedicated.

13. 1 mark for any valid answer, e.g.
- Andrew pestered his parents
- His dad was keen on bikes
- His parents knew he was serious about it

14. 1 mark for any valid **similarity**, e.g.
- The texts are both about people dedicated to their activity.
- Both texts describe the excitement people find in challenging situations.

1 mark for a valid explanation of **how this feature affects the reader**, e.g.
- It encourages the reader to respect / admire the people described.
- It helps the reader understand how people who do extreme sports feel about what they do.

1 mark for any valid **difference**, e.g.
- *Going Up* goes into a lot more detail about how the writer feels. Uses more descriptive and emotive language. The *Mountain Bike Champion* interview is chattier and focuses more on the physical side of the sport.
- *Going Up* is from the point of view of a beginner, but *Mountain Bike Champion* tells you the views of someone who has won a medal and is very experienced.

1 mark for any valid explanation of **how the difference affects the reader**, e.g.
- *Going Up* makes the reader feel more personally involved. It is more exciting to read because it talks about the climb, and the climber's feelings as she did it, in detail. *Mountain Bike Champion* doesn't discuss the biker's feelings in much detail.
- You get very different perspectives on extreme sports from the two articles. The beginner who is slightly scared in *Going Up* has a different perspective to the experienced biker in *Mountain Bike Champion*.

Writing Paper — Section A — Sets A, B & C

There are some really helpful points about marking
on page 293— make sure you read them first.

> You can use the same mark scheme to mark any of the Section A questions for
> **Sentence Structure and Punctuation** and **Text Structure and Organisation**
> (see below and on the next page). To mark questions for **Composition and Effect**,
> find the correct mark scheme for the specific question on pages 302-304.

Sentence Structure and Punctuation

WHAT'S THE ANSWER LIKE?	MARK
• Only makes use of simple connectives such as "and" / "but". • Noun phrases short and simple, e.g. "narrow streets". • Little or no use of pronouns and few attempts to vary vocabulary. • Little or no variation in punctuation — uses full stops and commas.	**0** marks
• Uses some more varied connectives to link parts of sentences, e.g. "although" or "because". • Some noun phrases expanded, but in a simple way, e.g. "narrow and winding streets". • Makes some attempts to use subordinate clauses, e.g. "Harry wasn't sure what to do next, so he sat down on a park bench to think about it." • Mostly simple verbs used in the present tense. • Attempts to use a range of punctuation, although this may be limited.	**1-2** marks
• Connectives more varied and used more confidently, sometimes developing a sentence beyond simple clause and subordinate clause, e.g. "Although Harry wasn't exactly sure what he should do with the money, he did know that he was going to enjoy spending every single penny…" • Uses expanding noun phrases such as "The narrow, winding streets at the centre of town are very old, possibly medieval…" • Some attempt to vary sentence starters, such as "If I were you" / "Maybe you shouldn't". • Punctuation mostly used correctly, and some variety shown, e.g. exclamation marks, brackets.	**3-4** marks
• Good use of a range of connectives such as "on the other hand" / "however". • Sentence length and type varied for effect, e.g. includes impersonal sentences like "It is important that..." • Good use of a wide range of punctuation.	**5-6** marks
• Good range of sentence starters, such as "On the other hand…" / "Some people think…" • Uses a good range of sentence constructions, varying length of clause / subclause for effect. • Can write in an impersonal tone to increase impact of text, e.g. "Many people say that…" • Makes use of a wide range of punctuation to good effect.	**7** marks
• Secure and confident control of sentences and their structure for maximum effect. • Uses a wide range of sentence constructions, e.g. rhetorical questions, complex sentences, concise sentences. • Uses the full range of punctuation effectively.	**8** marks

Now look at the next page and mark the piece for "Text Structure and Organisation"…

Writing Paper — Section A — Sets A, B & C

*There are some really helpful points about marking
on page 293 — make sure you read them first.*

Text Structure and Organisation

WHAT'S THE ANSWER LIKE?	MARK
• Very limited introduction or conclusion. • Very little structure, e.g. few or no paragraphs. • Some simple linking of ideas, e.g. "and then" / "also".	**0** marks
• Some clear attempt at a beginning, middle and end. • Some use of paragraphs to divide main groups of ideas. • Topic sentences used to introduce some paragraphs, e.g. "In the city centre there is a lot more to do…" • Some topic sentences developed into further ideas, but in a limited way.	**1-2** marks
• New ideas divided into paragraphs. • Some attempt to follow a structure, e.g. "You say you're thinking about running away… but I can't believe…" • Some more varied connectives used, such as "however" / "although". • Some development of ideas within paragraphs by giving examples or more detail.	**3-4** marks
• Paragraphs consistently linked with more complicated connectives such as "In addition to the leisure centre…" / "Finally, having finished the tennis match…" • Paragraphs introduced with a strong starter sentence, e.g. "The importance of comprehensive leisure facilities cannot be overstated." • Ideas within paragraphs more fully developed, e.g. by using supporting evidence.	**5-6** marks
• Paragraphs are all well organised to make the text clear and effective. • Connectives consistently and effectively used to develop points or arguments. • Discourse markers used to show stage of argument or piece, e.g. "At last…" or "Firstly, Alex…" • Variety of well thought out sentence structures within a paragraph, that flow effectively.	**7** marks
• Suitable number of paragraphs of a suitable length to constitute a clear argument. • Each paragraph follows the previous one smoothly and logically. • Complex topic sentences direct readers' attention to argument / ideas. • Paragraph content and structure consistently, carefully and confidently controlled for maximum effect.	**8** marks

*Now look at pages 302-304, and mark the piece for "Composition and Effect".
There are different mark schemes for each paper...*

Writing Paper — Section A — Set A

*There are some really helpful points about marking
on page 293 — make sure you read them first.*

Composition and Effect — Set A, Improving the Common Room

WHAT'S THE ANSWER LIKE?	MARK
• Little understanding of audience or purpose of the text. • Brief piece of writing with little detail and no developed ideas. • No attempt to explain the decisions.	**0** marks
• Attempts to organise ideas into paragraphs. • Some clear information on what has been done. • Gives some reasons for spending choices.	**1-3** marks
• Good opening paragraph which makes intentions clear. • Detailed information about several decisions with some reasons mentioned. • Appropriate choice of formal language.	**4-6** marks
• Report is well organised into distinct sections. • Describes details of spending with convincing reasons. • Clear sense of how students have benefited. • Consistent and appropriate formal tone.	**7-9** marks
• Clearly organised paragraphs which cover a variety of information. • Well-developed explanations of a range of decisions and outcomes. • Several benefits explained. • Good use of varied formal language appropriate to the audience.	**10-12** marks
• Report is well organised, with an easy-to-follow structure. • Interesting and realistic range of improvements and benefits mentioned. • Each decision / benefit is fully and clearly explained. • Confident, convincing formal tone conveys appreciation for the Parents' Association's help.	**13-14** marks

Writing Paper — Section A — Set B

There are some really helpful points about marking
on page 293— make sure you read them first.

Composition and Effect — Set B, Teen Readers

WHAT'S THE ANSWER LIKE?	MARK
• Little understanding of the audience or the purpose of the task. • Brief piece of writing with few details or ideas. • No attempt to use the conventions of a report.	**0** marks
• Some attempt to tackle the purpose of the writing. • Some awareness that the report should be formal. • Some details about why teenagers might not like the library and / or how they could be encouraged to use it more.	**1-3** marks
• Fairly good opening paragraph that shows awareness of the purpose of the report. • Some good use of formal language appropriate for the purpose, e.g. "In my opinion" • Some points developed well with more detail and information, e.g. "Furthermore, Smithtown library has seen numbers rise because..." • Offers some evidence to support ideas, such as made-up quotations from teenagers.	**4-6** marks
• Clearly addresses audience and purpose of task. • Uses a consistently appropriate tone for advising, e.g. "I really believe that if we offer this we will see more teenagers coming through our doors". • Consistent use of formal language appropriate to a report for a boss. • Several detailed points and ideas with developed supporting evidence. • Clearly organised into paragraphs or sections.	**7-9** marks
• Convincing report which fulfils its objectives. • Well organised into paragraphs that follow on logically and clearly from one another, e.g. using signposts such as "In addition to these points..." • Makes confident and varied use of supporting evidence such as made-up quotations, personal stories or statistics. • Tone, style and language are appropriate and effective throughout.	**10-12** marks
• Well organised, realistic and easy-to-follow report which fulfils its objectives. • All points fully developed with a variety of supporting evidence used when appropriate. • Convincing and successful use of formal tone throughout. • Varied and interesting use of formal language appropriate for advising a boss.	**13-14** marks

Writing Paper — Section A — Set C

*There are some really helpful points about marking
on page 293— make sure you read them first.*

Composition and Effect — Set C, Bad Behaviour

WHAT'S THE ANSWER LIKE?	MARK
• Little understanding of the audience or the purpose of the text. • Little written with few details or ideas shown. • No attempt to use conventions of a formal letter.	**0** marks
• Attempts to tackle the purpose of the writing. • Some awareness that the letter should be formal, e.g. "I understand that you have written to our head teacher..." • Some examples of persuasive writing, such as "I'm sure you agree..."	**1-3** marks
• Good opening paragraph that sets out the purpose of the letter. • Fairly good use of formal language. Not always consistent. • Some points developed well with more detail and information, e.g. "One example of the things we do for the local community is providing entertainment at the local old people's home..." • Some awareness of appropriate tone to persuade an older person.	**4-6** marks
• Clearly addresses audience and purpose of task. • Appropriate tone. • Consistent use of formal language that is respectful to the elderly lady. • Some detailed points and ideas with developed supporting evidence. • Clearly organised into paragraphs.	**7-9** marks
• Persuasive and realistic letter. • Well organised into paragraphs that follow on logically and clearly from one another, using signposts such as "Consequently..." or "However..." • Points supported by varied and persuasive evidence. • Tone, style and language appropriate and effective throughout.	**10-12** marks
• Effective, realistic and easy-to-follow letter. • Fully developed, interesting points supported with detailed evidence. • Persuasive but respectful tone throughout. • Varied and interesting use of formal language appropriate for a letter.	**13-14** marks

Writing Paper — Section B — Sets A, B & C

There are some really helpful points about marking
on page 293 — make sure you read them first.

You can use the same mark scheme to mark any of the Section B questions for **Spelling** and **Sentence Structure, Punctuation and Text Organisation**. To mark questions for **Composition and Effect**, find the correct mark scheme for the specific question on pages 306-307.

Spelling

WHAT'S THE ANSWER LIKE?	MARK
• Simple words of one syllable spelt correctly. • Common words of more than one syllable spelt correctly, e.g. because. • Some words confused, e.g. here / hear. • Some words spelt as they sound, e.g. secondry instead of secondary.	**1** mark
• Most words that follow a regular pattern spelt correctly. • Some more difficult words spelt incorrectly, e.g. rec<u>ie</u>ve instead of rec<u>ei</u>ve. • Some prefixes and suffixes spelt incorrectly, e.g. di<u>ss</u>appeared instead of di<u>s</u>appeared.	**2** marks
• Most words spelt correctly, including unusual words. • Some minor mistakes such as unstressed vowels missed out, e.g. diffrent instead of different. • Occasional mistakes with more difficult words.	**3** marks
• Almost every word spelt perfectly. • Any very minor slips are rare and not repeated.	**4** marks

Sentence Structure, Punctuation and Text Organisation

WHAT'S THE ANSWER LIKE?	MARK
• Makes use of only very simple connectives, such as "and". • Makes no use of pronouns (e.g. he, she, it). • Most sentences constructed correctly, but basic. • Makes little or no use of punctuation beyond full stops and commas.	**0** marks
• Sometimes uses simple subordinate clauses to extend sentences, e.g. "<u>Though you may get slightly uncomfortable</u>, all the money we raise will go to a good charitable cause." • Makes use of modal verbs, like "might", "may", "could" etc. • Beginning to use more complex sentences. • Sentences grouped together with the same topic. • More varied use of punctuation, but still limited.	**1-2** marks
• Longer and more complex sentences including some with several parts. • Makes use of more complex verb forms, e.g. imperatives such as "Beware!" • Sentences organised into paragraphs. • Points developed within paragraphs. • Punctuation used correctly and with some variety.	**3-4** marks
• Sustained use of complex sentences. • Sentence length and style varied for effect. • Range of connectives used effectively and confidently, both in sentences and between paragraphs — e.g. "You will need to perform for 15 minutes, <u>so</u> make sure you have enough material." • Paragraphs clearly organised and flow smoothly. • Variety of punctuation used confidently and successfully.	**5** marks
• Able to use a range of verb forms consistently and successfully, including the passive voice to maintain an impersonal tone, where appropriate — e.g. "the changes <u>were well received</u>." • Points clearly and thoroughly developed. • Topic sentences used to begin paragraphs and paragraphs organised carefully for maximum effect. • Confident use of varied punctuation to good effect.	**6** marks

Answers

Writing Paper — Section B — Set A

*There are some really helpful points about marking
on page 293— make sure you read them first.*

Composition and Effect — Set A, Summer Fair Fundraising

WHAT'S THE ANSWER LIKE?	MARK
• Little or no awareness of audience or purpose of text. • No use made of information in the prompt. • No attempt to engage interest through choice of language.	**0** marks
• Some awareness of writing for teaching staff. • Attempts to give reasons why they should volunteer. • A few attempts to sound persuasive, e.g. "You ought to volunteer"; "We need you to volunteer"; "It will be good".	**1-3** marks
• Sounds quite convincing with friendly but polite tone. • Several reasons for volunteering are given. • Vocabulary varied for persuasive effect, e.g. "this rare opportunity"; "star in the summer fair spectacular".	**4-6** marks
• Tone is light-hearted but still formal enough for staff audience. • A good range of convincing reasons to volunteer given. • Several persuasive devices used, e.g. rhetorical questions, examples, sets of three, statistics, emotive language.	**7-9** marks
• Well controlled tone of friendly persuasion, humour and the appropriate level of formality. • Intelligent use made of information in the prompt. • Uses a wide range of persuasive devices, e.g. anticipating staff response with counter-argument such as "You'll probably get wet but the water is nice and warm." • Well argued piece of writing which flows and is easy to read.	**10** marks

Writing Paper — Section B — Sets B&C

Composition and Effect — Set B, Talent Contest

WHAT'S THE ANSWER LIKE?	MARK
• Little awareness shown of audience or purpose of text. • No attempt to address points suggested in the task. • Little written and little to attract readers' interest.	**0** marks
• Some awareness shown of the task's audience and purpose. • Some attempts to offer simple information relating to the talent contest. • Some use of effective vocabulary and some simple noun phrases, e.g. "The talent show will be an exciting competition."	**1-3** marks
• Good awareness of the task's audience and purpose. • Uses a range of devices to inform the audience about the talent contest and keep them interested. • Covers the ideas suggested in the task, with some developed in more detail.	**4-6** marks
• Makes an effort to catch the audience's attention from the beginning. • Well organised and informative writing. • Good use of devices, such as subheadings, to interest and inform the reader. • Appropriate use of informal language.	**7-9** marks
• Convincing and realistic leaflet that is appropriate for its audience and purpose. • Well organised and easy to follow, with varied and helpful stylistic devices. • Detailed and well developed points. • Confidently written.	**10** marks

Composition and Effect — Set C, Relaxation Area

WHAT'S THE ANSWER LIKE?	MARK
• Little or no awareness of audience or purpose of text. • No attempt to provide the information requested in the task. • Little written and little attempt to describe a new relaxation area.	**0** marks
• Some awareness shown of task's audience and purpose. • Some attempts to describe the relaxation area, but little detail. • Some simple noun phrases such as, "The room should have comfortable seats. The room should have music playing in it."	**1-3** marks
• Some good awareness of the task's audience and purpose. • Suggested ideas are tackled more thoroughly, for example, "I'd like to see lilac walls with some artwork dotted around." • Uses varied language and descriptive devices. • Covers fully the requested information with some developed information where appropriate.	**4-6** marks
• Good awareness of the task's audience and purpose. • Interesting and descriptive piece of writing. • Varied use of devices such as rhetorical questions, emotive language and detail to interest the reader. • Sentences fully developed.	**7-9** marks
• Enjoyable and convincing descriptive writing, suitable for its audience and purpose. • Lots of original descriptive detail that avoids cliché. • Well organised, varied and imaginative. • Developed in an appropriate and well-controlled way.	**10** marks

Shakespeare Papers

There are some really helpful points about marking
on page 293 — make sure you read them first.

1) Count up the number of separate points made to answer the essay question. On the appropriate grid, tick one box for each point (up to 6 ticks).

2) Tick one box for every one of those points that's backed up by a quote (up to 6 ticks).

3) Then tick one box for every point that's expanded with a comment (up to 6 ticks).

4) Finally count up all the ticks to give a mark out of 18.

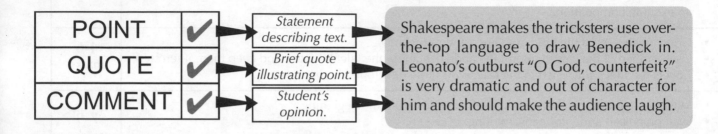

POINT	✔	→	Statement describing text.	→	Shakespeare makes the tricksters use over-the-top language to draw Benedick in. Leonato's outburst "O God, counterfeit?" is very dramatic and out of character for him and should make the audience laugh.
QUOTE	✔	→	Brief quote illustrating point.		
COMMENT	✔	→	Student's opinion.		

Set A — Shakespeare Paper

POINT	✔					
QUOTE						
COMMENT						

Set B — Shakespeare Paper

POINT	✔					
QUOTE						
COMMENT						

Set C — Shakespeare Paper

POINT	✔					
QUOTE						
COMMENT						

SMEB34